Basics of Law Librarianship

Haworth Series on Special Librarianship

Series Editor: Ellis Mount

Basics of Law Librarianship

Deborah S. Panella

The Haworth Press
New York • London

Basics of Law Librarianship is Volume Number 2 in the Haworth Series in Special Librarianship.

The Haworth Press, Inc. 10 Alice Street, Binghamton, NY 13904-1580
EUROSPAN/Haworth, 3 Henrietta Street, London WC2E 8LU England

Library of Congress Cataloging-in-Publication Data

Panella, Deborah S.

    Basics of law librarianship / Deborah S. Panella.
       p. cm. – (Haworth series in special librarianship : v. 2)
    Includes bibliographical references (p.) and index.
    ISBN 0-86656-989-8. – ISBN 0-86656-990-1 (pbk.)
    1. Law libraries – Handbooks, manuals, etc. 2. Law libraries – Administration. I. Title.
II. Series.
Z675.L2P36   1990
026.34 – dc20
                                                       90-4898
                                                         CIP

CONTENTS

ALL HAWORTH BOOKS & JOURNALS
ARE PRINTED ON CERTIFIED
ACID-FREE PAPER

ABOUT THE AUTHOR

Deborah S. Panella, MLS, has ten years of experience in law librarianship. She is presently Managing Librarian for the law firm of Paul, Weiss, Rifkind, Wharton & Garrison in New York where she supervises a library staff of 40 that serves nearly 400 lawyers. She has written several articles on law librarianship which have appeared in the *National Law Journal, Legal Economics,* and *Legal Administrator*, and she contributed a chapter to the book *Creative Planning of Special Library Facilities* (The Haworth Press, 1988). Ms. Panella is a member of several professional associations, including the American Association of Law Libraries, the Special Libraries Association, the American Society for Information Science, and the Association for Information and Image Management.

Series Editor's Comments

The topic of this book, law librarianship, is a particularly welcome addition to the Haworth Series in Special Librarianship for several reasons. One is the lack of much information in book form on the operation of law libraries. Another is the importance of law libraries to the profession. Some of the most significant events in modern society hinge on the role played by lawyers. It would seem to follow that the better served they are by their libraries, the better the decisions they would make in their professional dealings.

The book's author, Deborah Panella, is admirably suited to write such a book since she has served as Head Librarian for several years for a large, prominent New York law firm. It should be evident from reading the book that she has written on the basis of experience gained by working in a challenging environment.

Ellis Mount

Acknowledgements

Special thanks to Marsha Stein and Andreas Antoniou who offered constant encouragement and support. Their advice and assistance made this possible. Thanks are also in order for Jean O'Grady, who read the final manuscript and offered sound suggestions which are incorporated throughout. Finally, special thanks to the staff of the Library and Word Processing Departments at Paul, Weiss for their help in obtaining the resources and typing the manuscript.

This book is dedicated to John and our daughters, Dana, Caitlin and Robin, with love.

Acknowledgments

Chapter 1

The History and Nature
of Law Libraries

HISTORY OF LAW LIBRARIES

The history of law libraries has been well researched and reported.[1] Law libraries of limited scope have existed since ancient
times, when priests memorized the few "written" law books and
preserved the original works. In this country, law libraries existed
even in colonial times. They began as the private collections of
individual lawyers. Until the 19th century, they actually contained
few law books. Most "law" collections actually consisted of books
on philosophy, ethics, history, politics, and the social sciences. The
few law titles in these collections were, in fact, English law books,
and a library of 10-20 volumes was considered to be a good library.
Although there are references to law books as early as the mid-
1600s, less than 30 law books had actually been published in America by 1776. The first volume of cases from United States courts
was published in 1789, and in 1885, nearly 100 years later, there
were still only 3,798 volumes of law reports. Today, there are over
65,000 cases reported annually by West Publishing Company alone,
resulting in over 3,000,000 cases available through West. Their
National Reporter System alone increases by over 200 volumes annually.

The development of shared law libraries followed shortly after
U.S. law reports began to be published, but the Library of Congress
was not really the first such library. In 1800, the Library of Congress was established for the President, Vice President, and members of Congress, although the Justices of the Supreme Court were
not allowed to use it until 1812. Not until 1832 was the law book

collection segregated, and not until 1873 was the Supreme Court Library established as a separate facility for use by the Justices.

The first known organized law library in the United States was the Law Library Company of Philadelphia, formed in 1802. Members purchased stock at $20 per share, which enabled them to use the law collection and to socialize with other prestigious members of the company. Shortly thereafter, in 1804, Boston's Social Law Library was formed, requiring a subscription fee for access to the collection. Similar institutions across the country were then established, including the New York Law Institute (1824), the Detroit Library (1838), the Chicago Law Institute (1839), and the Association of the Bar of the City of New York (1870).

The earliest public law library, the Allegheny County Law Library in Belmont, New York, started in 1806. State and county law libraries were usually part of the state library system rather than independent facilities and collections, so their history is difficult to track. Most seem to have developed during the mid-1800s.

The first known law school library, that of Harvard University, was established in 1817 when the school established a separate law department and law book collection as part of the library. As late as 1900, however, only six law school libraries existed. Law school students elsewhere were expected to use practitioners' libraries.

Even the practicing lawyers' libraries at this point remained libraries of private individuals. The private law firm library, or corporate practice library, developed in the early 1900s.

Law librarians, of course, are even newer than any of these law libraries. The first libraries were developed, maintained, and organized by the lawyers themselves. As the collections grew and the interests of the members expanded, it became necessary for a caretaker to be hired. This person was usually trained in the law rather than in library science, a tradition that has been hard to break. In part, having a librarian trained in the law was due to the legal profession's belief that only lawyers could read and organize a law collection. Of course, another factor was that the first school of Library Science did not open until 1887, when Melvil Dewey began the Columbia School of Library Service.

As early as 1899, the Cravath law firm in New York had hired a file clerk who had been trained at the Columbia University Library. Law schools began to hire librarians in the 1920s, and by 1950, the one-person library was quite common. As late as 1972, however, a survey of law firm libraries indicated that approximately half of the librarians were lawyers, and half were graduates of library science programs. Even today, although the library degree is required for nearly all librarian positions in public and academic institutions, many other law library positions can be filled instead by lawyers or nonprofessionals. Conversely, in law school libraries, many positions now require both the library and law degrees. Today the American Association of Law Libraries boasts a membership of over 4,100 law librarians.

TYPES OF LAW LIBRARIES

The easiest way to distinguish among various types of law libraries is to describe their clientele, for that provides the essence of the differences among the libraries themselves. There are law libraries that serve the private sector (private law firm and corporate legal department libraries), those that serve law students (academic law libraries), those that serve practicing lawyers in the community (bar association libraries), and those that serve judges and lawyers and the public in legal districts (court, county, and state law libraries). There are also governmental libraries, such as the Department of Justice Library, and special libraries in correctional institutions to serve the inmate population. Obviously, these categories are not clear cut; many law libraries actually serve more than one population. For example, many state, county, and court libraries serve judges, practicing lawyers, and the public, and could therefore be considered public law libraries, while others have more restricted use. Nonetheless, the categorical breakdown of law libraries allows us to compare and contrast their operations and to illustrate the variety of law library responsibilities.

Private Law Libraries

The private law library is generally a department within a law firm or private law practice. The largest law firms now have more than 1,000 lawyers, with legal practices in nearly all fields of law. Furthermore, they may have branch offices nationally and internationally. The libraries that exist to meet the needs of these megafirms may be quite large, with annual budgets greater than $1 million, staffs of 25 or 30, and branch libraries in other domestic or foreign cities. Perhaps more common, though, is the one-person or one-professional library, serving a small to mid-sized law firm. In fact, many private law libraries still exist without any librarian because they are small enough to be maintained by the lawyers, paralegals, or secretarial support within the firm or law office. Also in this category of private law libraries are corporate law libraries, which support the in-house legal staff within a company or corporation. As with law firm libraries, their size varies greatly, although they rarely reach the size of the major law firm libraries.

A feature of the private law library is the emphasis on obtaining obscure or massive amounts of information, often in a hurry, and often without regard to the cost. This "no holds barred" approach to research requests means that most librarians are creative and resourceful researchers who can remain efficient and effective under a high degree of stress. This environment is intolerable to those who like to teach, however, since emphasis is clearly on providing the answer rather than explaining how to do it.

Another feature is the collection's currency. Few private collections contain much historical law material. Their emphasis is on the practical needs; that is, the tools needed to practice law today. Theoretical and developmental materials are rarely found in abundance in private law collections, and the actual collections will vary tremendously from library to library. There are no minimum standards for the private law firm or corporate legal department library, since they exist solely to support the needs of the parent organization.

Based on an unofficial count of libraries listed in the *1989-90 AALL Directory and Handbook*,[2] the American Association of Law Libraries counts among its members over 850 law firm libraries and 125 corporate legal department libraries. Over half of the membership of AALL is now made up of librarians in law firms and corporations.

Academic Law Libraries

All law schools in the United States have law libraries to support the research needs of the faculty and students of the institution. The American Bar Association and the Association of American Law

Schools have set minimum standards for the collections and staff of accredited law schools. Institutions whose libraries do not meet the minimum standards will lose their accreditation. Standards for the Approval of Law Schools were first developed in 1881 by the American Bar Association's Section of Legal Education and Admission to the Bar. Since then, the standards have been amended numerous times to reflect the changing expectations and demands of the legal profession.

One significant feature of academic law libraries is their emphasis on research, both historical and theoretical. These collections include many ancient and colonial documents which form the basis of our Constitution and laws today. These collections are intended to support the needs of faculty and students for critical review and analysis of law systems. For example, comparative legal materials describing similar laws and legal systems of various countries abound in law school libraries, although they are less frequently found elsewhere.

Most academic law libraries today are faced with tremendous collection development problems. The proliferation of published law reports and treatises has made selection a difficult problem and resource sharing a necessity. Between 1960 and 1970, the collections of the ten largest law school libraries grew 42%, but the rate of growth among the more established law libraries has declined since then.[3] While major law libraries used to take pride in their exhaustive collections, these research institutions have become more selective in their purchases as legal publishing continues to flourish.

In a growing number of law school libraries, the library directors have both the library and the law degree. Librarians in academic environments are often required to publish, and they are often the standard-setters for the rest of the law librarian profession.

There are nearly 200 law school libraries listed in the *1989-90 AALL Directory and Handbook*. In 1986, the average academic law library collection consisted of 264,349 volumes. The largest law school library, at Harvard University, contained 1,565,926 volumes, compared with the smallest reported law school library with 71,105 volumes. The average number of full-time professionals on the staff was 10, with a high of 32.7 and a low of 2. The largest law school library budget was $4,128,227, while the smallest was $76,844.[4] The percentage of law school budgets devoted to the law school library is presently about 18%, as it has been for at least the last ten years.[5]

Bar Association Libraries

Bar association libraries began as private social associations supported by membership contributions or subscriptions. Many of these associations were essentially private clubs, and their collections and services varied depending upon the needs of their members. The bar associations today are open to any lawyers who are admitted to practice in a geographic area (usually a court district). Today's bar association libraries still vary in size and scope, depending upon the funds available from the members of the bar and their members' influence in determining the collection focus. Most of these libraries combine an excellent historical collection from private donations as well as their own early histories (which often pre-date academic law libraries) with vast reference collections for practitioners. These bar libraries serve all members of the parent association, including individual lawyers and those affiliated with large law firms. Additionally, many judges and court clerks may use bar libraries to supplement the collections of the court libraries. In many bar libraries, books may not leave the premises, so material is always available to the library patron.

The staff in bar association libraries may consist of one librarian and a clerical assistant, or there may be large staffs of librarians and assistants. These librarians must often have knowledge of all fields to meet the needs of the variety of lawyers who use the library.

Government-Sponsored Law Libraries

Government-sponsored law libraries are widely varied in size and purpose. An unofficial count of the libraries in the *1989-90 AALL Directory and Handbook* indicated that there are presently over 200 such institutions. Supported by public funds, these federal, state, county, and court libraries are usually open to the public, but exist primarily to meet the needs of judges, lawyers, and government officials.

The largest group of government-sponsored law libraries is the court or county law library. Librarians in these libraries must handle various patrons, from the respected judge with 20 years on the bench to the citizen interested in suing his neighbor over a broken fence. There are nearly 400 individual members of the state, county, and court special interest section of AALL.

Another division of government library is that which meets the needs of a particular agency or department. Although these libraries are relatively few, they are an important group of law libraries. Among the most prominent of these are the libraries of the Department of Justice and the Securities and Exchange Commission.

One fairly distinct type of government-sponsored law library is the prison law library, which exists to serve the prison inmate population. Several court decisions have established guidelines for prison law libraries. In 1977, the Supreme Court of the United States, in Bounds v. Smith, 430 U.S. 817 (1977), stated that prison authorities were obligated to provide adequate law libraries or other forms of legal assistance. Although interpretations of this decision vary, many prison systems have improved their libraries since 1977, and other court decisions have attempted to define "adequate" contents of law libraries. Many associations, including the American Association of Law Libraries and the American Bar Association have addressed prisoners' needs as well.[6]

Prison law libraries are often not staffed by a professional librarian. Most are staffed by corrections officers, volunteers, or the inmates themselves. Although some prison law libraries contain adequate core collections, they remain inadequate because the staff lacks training in their use and updating requirements. In some jurisdictions, the on-site collections are quite small, and inmates rely on county law libraries or the law school library interlibrary loan process.

There are at least 10 correctional institution libraries listed in the *1989-90 AALL Directory and Handbook*, none of which holds more than 10,000 volumes. Although many more prison law libraries exist, their representation in the association remains small because few such libraries are professionally staffed.

Public Law Libraries

The public library in most communities today rarely has many law books. Well-developed law collections are extremely expensive and could easily use up a community's annual library budget. Furthermore, the legal profession has always felt that although legal materials should be available to all, only lawyers are qualified to interpret them and render legal advice. Therefore, some public library boards and librarians have felt compelled to avoid the purchase of legal titles to avoid the claim that they could then be professionally or personally liable for giving incomplete or incorrect "legal advice." As with the medical field, people are discouraged from self-diagnosis and are encouraged to seek a professional's help. In recent years, a number of courses have been developed to teach legal research skills to non-law librarians, possibly indicating a trend toward basic legal research competency among a broader range of librarians.

REFERENCE NOTES

1. The subject of law libraries is well documented in many sources. For those used in researching this chapter, see the following annotated bibliography.
2. Butler, Anne H.; Peterson, Randall T.; Wolfe, Bardie C. Jr. *AALL Directory and Handbook, 1989-90*. 29th ed. Chicago, IL: Published for the American Association of Law Libraries by Commerce Clearing House, Inc.; 1989.
3. Mersky, Roy M.; Jacobstein, J. Myron. An analysis of academic law library growth since 1907. *Law Library Journal*. 75:212-224; 1982.
4. Thomas, David A. 1985-86 statistical survey of law school libraries and librarians. *Law Library Journal*. 79: 547-596; 1987.
5. Hammond, Jane L. Library costs as a percentage of law school budgets. *Law Library Journal*. 80:439-445; 1988.
6. See, for example: American Association of Law Libraries. Committee on Law Library Service to Prisoners. *Recommended collections for prisons and other institution law libraries*. Rev. ed. Chicago, IL: AALL; 1976; American Bar Association. Resource Center on Correctional Law and Legal Services. *Providing legal services to prisoners*. Chicago, IL: ABA; 1973; National Advisory Commission on Criminal Justice Standards and Goals. *Report on corrections. Standard 2.3: Access to legal materials*. Washington: The Commission; 1973: 29-30.

BIBLIOGRAPHY

A Symposium of law publishers, *American Law Review*. 23: 396; 1889 as reprinted in: A Second look. *Legal Reference Services Quarterly*. 1(4):73-91; 1981 Winter.
    This 100-year-old symposium sheds light on the development of the case reporting system we know today.

Brock, Christine A. Law libraries and librarians: a revisionist history, or more than you ever wanted to know. *Law Library Journal*. 67(3):325-361; 1974.

Excellent history of law libraries and librarians, with subdivisions by type of library. Filled with interesting details, and the best article on the topic.

Ellenberger, J.S. History and development of the modern law library in the United States. *In*: Mueller and Kehoe, eds., *Law librarianship: a handbook*. Littleton, Co.: Rothman; 1983:1-12.

Interesting and readable introduction to law library history. Most interesting are the statistics and comments regarding the rapid, nearly uncontrollable, growth of law publishing.

Mersky, Roy M., moderator. Bicentennial history of American law libraries. *Law Library Journal*. 69(4): 528-553; 1976.

A symposium held at the American Association of Law Libraries annual meeting. The speakers' presentations were informative and carefully referenced for anyone wishing to research the topic more fully.

Morehead, Joe. All cases great and small: the West Publishing Company saga. *Serials Librarian*. 14(1/2):3-17; 1988.

A look at the history and development of West Publishing Company.

Parrish, Jenni. Law books and legal publishing in America, 1760-1840. *Law Library Journal*. 72(3): 355-452; 1979.

The author identifies 509 monographs published in America between 1760 and 1840, indicating that "the impression we have of little or no legal publishing activity" is not entirely accurate. A very brief discussion of American legal education and publishing during that period is included.

Woxland, Thomas A. Forever associated with the practice of law: the early years of the West Publishing Company. *Legal Reference Services Quarterly*. 5(1):115-124; 1985 Spring.

An interesting look at the development of West Publishing Company, the largest publisher of case law in the United States, and the impact its policies and practices have had on the legal system.

Chapter 2

The Nature of the Legal Field
and the Legal Clientele

THE NATURE OF THE LEGAL CLIENTELE

The majority of law library users are lawyers, judges, legislators, or law school students. As previously stated, the general assumption on the part of lawyers (and surprisingly, also the public) is that only those trained in the law are qualified to read and interpret legal books. One indication of this is that most law books, and certainly legislation and contracts, are written in "legalese." The result is that the majority of law library patrons are highly educated, intelligent individuals. Their expectations and demands are high; these are not people who will be satisfied with partial or incorrect answers. Having been trained to think on their feet, to analyze, to challenge, and to cross-examine, they can be a difficult group to satisfy.

One of the reasons they are so demanding is that anything less than perfection may negatively affect the outcome of a court decision or influence a legal argument. The positions lawyers take and the arguments they make are based on the information they have collected. The resultant court decisions have a significant impact on the people involved, and, in some cases, set precedent for future decisions. Therefore, just as it is necessary for a lawyer to collect all the facts surrounding an accident, it is essential that the lawyer also have all the relevant laws, regulations, and similar court decisions to be fully prepared to represent that accident victim. Furthermore, it may be helpful to have laws from other jurisdictions to challenge the law in the victim's state. Non-legal research is also important, since perhaps research will show that the automobile manufacturer knew of a brake defect.

As we are all aware, some court decisions are a matter of life and death, and far more decisions have an impact on people's quality of life. With such responsibilities in their hands, it is no wonder that lawyers have the reputation of being demanding library patrons.

THE NATURE OF LEGAL RESEARCH TOOLS

To understand how American legal research tools are organized, it is helpful to understand the basic arrangement of our legal system. The legal system of the United States is based on a common law tradition that originated and developed in England. In a common law system, the law of the land is set by statute as well as by precedent.[1] Statutes, commonly called laws, are acts of the legislature that "prescribe conduct, define crimes, create inferior governmental bodies, appropriate public monies, and in general . . . promote the public good and welfare." Precedents are previous examples of the outcome of similar cases or questions of law and are used as authority. Our legal system uses precedents to adhere to the doctrine of *stare decisis*, which in Latin means "to stand by that which was decided." Simply stated, our courts base their decisions on the applicable laws and on what the courts of the same jurisdiction have ruled under similar circumstances in the past. In the United States, the common law system has become somewhat diluted as increasing numbers of statutes are enacted.

In that framework, legal literature is divided into two types of information: primary and secondary. Primary sources include statutes, administrative regulations, constitutional provisions, and court opinions (case law). Primary authority may then be defined as either binding or persuasive. The Constitution is binding, as are the laws and the highest court's decisions, in a given jurisdiction. In other words, a given court must follow the law set out in the jurisdiction's constitutional provisions, its legislation, and its highest courts' decisions. Persuasive authority consists of the laws and court decisions from other jurisdictions that would influence a given court, although the court is not required to follow them.

Secondary authority is never binding on the courts. All other legal literature, including textbooks, treatises, periodicals, practice manuals, and similar material, which describes, explains, or recommends legal developments, does not carry the same degree of importance in the courts. Some of these secondary sources are influential, however, and may be used in the lawmaking process or in the interpretation of laws within the courts. Many excellent treatises have been cited in courts' opinions, although they are not primary authority.

Morris Cohen identifies a third type of legal literature, distinct from primary and secondary materials, which he calls finding tools.[2] These are search aids, such as citators, indexes, digests, and other materials that are used to locate both primary and secondary materials. These finding aids have always been an important focus of legal research, due to the complexity of both our legal system and the related body of published legal materials. A legal researcher must first define his jurisdiction, both in terms of territory and subject matter, and then locate the relevant statutes, regulations, and case law. This task requires a sophistication rarely found in the novice.

One illustration of legal literature's complexity is the sheer number of legal research guides on the market.[3] Each of the more than 20 such books available today offers some unique features, and, as Danner points out, "the intended audience for the texts is broader than the traditional one of law students and librarians."

Another is the number of articles published on methods and problems associated with teaching legal research.[4] Many of the authors describe a dissatisfaction with the level of research skills held by today's law students and lawyers.

Legal literature suffers from some other problems caused by the legal system as well. One problem is that the body of legal literature is constantly growing. Not only are new materials (especially cases) being published, but in most situations the old ones are not withdrawn. The result is that there is an expanding core collection which must be consulted.

In a similar vein, statutory materials present numerous problems to the legal researcher. Legislative bodies are constantly enacting new laws which enhance, refine, or replace others. New laws governing previously uncharted territory (biological testing and genetic research, for example) are also developing. Having the most current version of statutes then becomes a key component of effective legal research, and not an easy one.

Another difficulty in legal research, especially for the non-lawyer, is understanding the terminology and grammar that are unique to legal writing. Despite the efforts of some for "plain language statutes," "legalese" is not likely to disappear.[5,6] Some would argue that the reason for this indecipherable body of writing is that the ability to read it separates the legal experts from the rest of the world. In fact, many statutes and cases are carefully—painstakingly—written to avoid misinterpretation.

Even with the focus on precise wording, yet another feature of legal research is the importance of background material. Legislative history, which consists of debates, reports, legislative drafts and revisions, and other historical material, is often reviewed to assist the lawyers and judges in determining not only what the law says, but what the legislators meant the statute to say. These supporting documents are used to infer how the resultant statute was intended to be used.

All of these factors have made it difficult for almost everyone, including the law librarian and lawyer, to do exhaustive legal research.

REFERENCE NOTES

1. Definitions are from: Gifis, Steven H. *Law dictionary*. 2nd ed. Woodbury, NY: Barron's; 1984.

2. Cohen, Morris L. Introduction. *In: Legal research in a nutshell*. 4th ed. St. Paul, MN: West Publishing Co.; 1985: p. 1-8.

3. For a discussion of the relative merits of each legal research guide, see: Snyder, Fritz. Review essay: legal research books, manuals and guides—more than enough. *Law Library Journal*. 80(3):307-328; 1988 and Danner, Richard A. From the editor: reading legal research. *Law Library Journal*. 79(1):1-6; 1979.

4. See, for example: Wren, Christopher G.; Wren, Jill Robinson. The teaching of legal research. *Law Library Journal*. 80(1):7-61; 1988 and Kauffman, S. Blair. Advanced legal research courses: a new trend in American legal education. *Legal Reference Services Quarterly*. 6(3/4): 123-139; Fall/Winter 1986.

5. Lloyd, Harold A. Plain language statutes: plain good sense or plain nonsense? *Law Library Journal*. 78(4):683-696; 1986
6. Sastri, M. I. Legalese revisited. *Law Library Journal*. 80(2):193-215; 1988.

BIBLIOGRAPHY

Berring, Robert C. How to be a great reference librarian. *Legal Reference Services Quarterly*. 4(1):17-37; 1984 Spring.
    The author presents his recommended book list for law librarians to become great reference librarians. The emphasis here is on historical reference tools, trivia, fact-finding resources, and current awareness titles.
Cohen, Morris L. Introduction. *In:* Legal research in a nutshell. 4th ed. St. Paul, MN: West; 1985:1-8.
    Morris Cohen, Law Librarian at Harvard, divides legal literature into three categories. In addition to primary and secondary materials, Cohen defines search books and finding tools as a distinct group of legal literature consisting of bibliographies, citators, digests, indexes, and similar materials.
Danner, Richard A. From the editor: reading legal research. *Law Library Journal*. 79(1):1-6; 1987.
    This brief article reviews six legal research books published in 1986 and presents a few of the author's views on what constitutes a good legal research text.
Gifis, Steven H. *Law dictionary*. 2nd ed. Woodbury, NY: Barron's; 1984.
    This paperback legal dictionary defines over 3,000 legal terms. Definitions are intended for law students, legal professionals, "and anyone else who deals with legal terminology" with "anyone else" being a key phrase. This legal dictionary is easily understood. The terms are clearly defined and explained.
Jacobstein, J. Myron; Mersky, Roy M. Glossary of terms and Ch. 1, The legal process. *In:* Fundamentals of legal research. 3rd ed. Mineola, NY: Foundation Press; 1985:xxi-xlvi and 1-9.
    Among the best treatises in legal research, this text is written by two of the most prominent law librarians in this country. The authors avoid "legalese," enabling the reader to easily understand difficult concepts identified in the glossary. Their introduction, though brief, concisely defines and describes primary v. secondary authority, thereby setting the stage for the rest of the chapters.
Lloyd, Harold A. Plain language statutes: plain good sense or plain nonsense? *Law Library Journal*. 78(4):683-696; 1986.
    The author describes the layman's complaints about legalese but presents an argument that plain language statutes will not replace the traditional "unclear, boring, haughty" legal language.
Sastri, M.I. Legalese revisited. *Law Library Journal*. 80(2):193-215; 1988.

The author explains why legalese is required and will not be replaced by "Plain English" and presents examples of famous legal writing.

Snyder, Fritz. Review essay: legal research books, manuals and guides—more than enough. *Law Library Journal*. 80(3):307-328; 1988.

The author reviews the merits and failures of 24 legal research texts, many of which have been published since 1980. Each book has been carefully and thoroughly reviewed for content, arrangement, and audience.

Stark, Steven. Why lawyers can't write. *Harvard Law Review*. 97(6):1389-1393; 1984.

This brief essay argues that lawyers write badly because they know too much and because it is in their best economic interests to do so.

Chapter 3

Collection Development

GROWING IMPORTANCE
OF COLLECTION DEVELOPMENT

One of the most difficult tasks for any law librarian today is collection development. "Collection development is a classic exercise in political economy. It is an attempt to allocate scarce resources — money, space and staff — among competing demands."[1] Always a time-consuming task, this aspect of law librarianship has become an increasingly complicated responsibility, requiring in-depth evaluation of choices. Some of the reasons for the increased focus on collection development are set forth below.

The Growth in Law Book Publishing

The proliferation of law books has resulted in enormous problems for even the largest law libraries in the country. Such libraries, whose policies once stated that they were to maintain "exhaustive" collections in certain fields of law, have been required to select books far more judiciously. The sheer number of new law books published annually has made it impossible to collect everything. Jacobstein and Mersky estimated that as of 1980 there were over 3,000,000 reported cases in the United States and that as many as 50,000 cases are reported annually in the various reporters.[2] There have been over 400 new legal serials published since 1980, while only 84 titles ceased publication during the same period.[3] Furthermore, periodicals have been larger and lengthier since 1960.[4]

Rising Costs of New Titles

Another problem is the escalating cost of purchasing a book. The average cost per legal continuation rose over $40 per title in just the last five years.[5] In 1984/85, the mean cost of a legal serial was $153.11, while the mean cost in 1988/89 was $197.49.

Supplementation Costs

Worse still is the cost of upkeep for law materials. Nearly every law library purchase requires not only an initial outlay but annual, quarterly, monthly, or more frequent supplementation to keep the title current. With laws and regulations constantly in a state of flux and the courts reporting record-breaking numbers of cases, it is dangerous and foolish for a library to keep outdated material on the shelves.

The Scope of Collections:
The Shrinking World

At one time, most law libraries collected legal materials related only to their geographic location or jurisdiction. Lawyers on the East Coast were only moderately interested in the legal developments on the West Coast. Today, the entire world is of interest. As with most other aspects of our lives, the law world as we see it is expanding and the boundaries are shrinking. Not only are we interested in the laws of the entire country but of the entire world. As business opportunities expand across the globe, so do disputes, and international conflict of laws has become an important issue to lawyers worldwide. Gaining access to the laws of all nations has become a major difficulty facing law librarians today. They are responding to the problem by identifying foreign contacts and book dealers and by putting increasing pressure on U.S. publishers to collect, translate, and publish the laws of foreign countries.

The Expanded Interest in Law-Related
and Non-Legal Titles

More and more law libraries have also found it necessary to collect at least a core collection of general or specialized non-legal reference and treatise materials. Many law librarians consider such titles as *Books in Print*, *Sheehy's Guide to Reference Books*, and Lorna Daniell's *Business Information Sources* required collection development tools.

THE ACQUISITIONS POLICY

It has been suggested that every law library have a written acquisitions policy, although as recently as 1983 they were rare. Reasons for the lack of such policies are: lack of budget problems (until recently); accountability rarely required, since the users' groups were satisfied; and the head librarian, being the primary or sole purchaser of materials, did not need written policy guidelines.[6] Today, the law librarian should consider implementation of such a policy as soon as possible.

ALTERNATIVES TO PURCHASING LEGAL MATERIALS

More and more, law libraries are relying upon the cooperation of others. Interlibrary loans are a part of daily life, and elaborate procedures and rules have been established. FAX machines have received wide acclaim as necessary library tools, and computer databases have made their way into all but the smallest facilities. LEXIS and Westlaw, the two major players in the full-text legal database arena, add new materials daily. The state of legal publishing has created such a demand for these pay-as-you-go systems that they can barely keep pace. Some law firms and other organizations are parts of groups that share libraries, commonly known as building libraries or cooperative libraries. Many of the smaller firms and solo practitioners rely heavily upon their bar association libraries or their county law libraries. Still others have access to the academic law library. Even so, it is fairly safe to say that there is not a library in the country that presently meets all of the needs of it patrons, and the future looks even more challenging.

Given limited space and budgetary constraints, the librarian in a small library must carefully evaluate the clientele and establish minimum needs. Consideration of alternative sources is essential. If a title is available on-line or at the local bar association library, it is possible that the library can do without it, unless it is a heavily used reference book or practice guide. Even large libraries need to question each new purchase carefully and to question that decision annually thereafter. All law librarians should be following the development of new technologies, such as CD-ROM, in the hope that it will assist with both space and budget problems of the future.

With a growing number of cases and statutes becoming available on LEXIS and Westlaw, the decision should also include a cost/benefit analysis of all alternatives. Before buying any book today, it is necessary to determine whether the library could borrow it, obtain it from on-line sources, or simply do without. Cost justification, however, is very complicated to do objectively. What are the effects of requiring the lawyer to wait for the information if it is not readily available? The librarian cannot simply base acquisitions decisions on the price.

SELECTION TOOLS

Because each law library's requirements are unique, no attempt to define a core collection will be made here. For some types of law libraries, minimum standards have been set by professional organizations. For example, academic law libraries must conform to guidelines established by the American Bar Association and by the Association of American Law Schools.[7]

Similarly, guidelines for prison law libraries were recommended by AALL in 1976,[8] and specific materials have been identified as essential by the American Correctional Association.[9]

CURRENT AWARENESS TOOLS

There are several excellent tools for collection development of law libraries. For some very small libraries, contact with the major legal publishers' representatives may be sufficient, but such instances are rare. Even if the librarians are unable to purchase titles, they would be wise to keep abreast of legal publications.

The following tools are the major resources consulted by law librarians today. The list is selective, but it is representative of the variety of resources available for acquiring American law materials.

Although they are fewer and more difficult to identify, similar resources exist for other countries, but are not included here.

Publishers' and Associations' Mailings

Being on the mailing lists for brochures and catalogs remains one of the best ways to stay abreast of new publications. Although the direct mailings always present titles in their best light, the astute librarian quickly learns to question all but the most highly respected legal publishers. The publishers are subject to FTC guidelines for announcements and advertisements. These guidelines, developed in the early 1970s, specifically require law book publishers to follow fair and honest practices. For example, brochures and advertisements must contain accurate publication dates and a history of supplementation cost.[10] In addition, the American Association of Law Libraries actively reports on the complaints lodged by librarians against the publishers. Finally, most publishers have an approval and return policy for the occasional misjudgment.

Word of Mouth

Both lawyers and other librarians are excellent resources. Lawyers or law professors specializing in a certain field or librarians responsible for collection development and reference can be trusted to know both what exists and what is needed.

Other Library Acquisitions Lists

Law libraries of all types publish new acquisitions lists, and many of these lists are free for the asking. A quick review of the new titles in a library of similar size, scope, and clientele will identify any titles that slipped through the cracks. Acquisitions of larger libraries will alert librarians to resources they may wish to know about for interlibrary loan purposes or to identify titles needed in their own library collections.

Current Publications in Legal and Related Fields

This monthly pamphlet, edited and published by Rothman for the American Association of Law Libraries, contains bibliographic and price information for law and law-related English language books and serials. It would be enhanced by subject arrangement, but it is a useful current awareness tool nonetheless.

Advance Bibliography of Law and Related Fields
Known as "Rothman's green slips," these weekly slips consist of bibliographic and price information for new law and law-related English language books and serials. The slip service allows acquisitions librarians to separate the slips for books of interest from the rest and to place orders by submitting the slips to Rothman to fulfill.

Bowker's Legal Publishing Preview
This newsletter, published six times a year, lists and reviews new and forthcoming legal books, periodicals, software, microforms, videotapes, and data bases.

Legal Information Alert
This newsletter, published ten times a year, contains announcements and reviews of new publications and databases in the legal field.

Practical Law Books Review
This quarterly newsletter, published by Library Management & Services (Austin, TX), is a "quick reference to new legal publications by field of specialization."

Book Reviews in Law Reviews
Many legal periodicals contain reviews of recently published law materials. Although the reviews in these journals may appear as much as one year after publication of the "new" material, these reviews can be very helpful in acquisitions decisions.

WEEDING

In law libraries, as in any other type of library, the word "weeding" elicits signs of guilt and anxiety. This is a task no one likes, and, since librarians can usually find value in any book, it is a painful challenge for them to discard anything. As previously mentioned, however, laws are constantly being replaced by new ones, and regulations are even more volatile. The fact is that law librarians have a great responsibility to remove outdated materials promptly. With some materials, the task is quite simple, since the updated version is sent automatically to the subscriber of the old. Instructions are clear on destruction or preservation for historical purposes of all prior editions. Unfortunately, this is not always the case. Frequently, it is the librarian's responsibility to identify and remove old legal materials. Because many law librarians are not lawyers, this can be a difficult task. It is rarely possible for a librarian to follow the law in any one field, not to mention the many fields most libraries collect. Simply knowing there has been a new law passed is, therefore, difficult. Additionally, one must determine whether or not the new law conflicts with the old ones. Oftentimes, new laws clarify or supplement those already in existence, so it is not necessary (nor wise) to remove treatises covering the older laws.

To further complicate matters, some laws that have been replaced by new ones are still valid under certain circumstances. For example, a survivor may be contesting the will of a relative who died many years ago. The laws in effect at the time of death may apply, even though newer ones are now in effect. Similarly, if a company declared bankruptcy in 1975, creditors may have been suing the company ever since that date. Even though new laws went into effect while the case was in court, the old laws apply. These are hypothetical examples intended only to illustrate the complications facing law librarians assigned to weeding the collection, but the fact is that such problems are quite common.

Unfortunately, it is rare for lawyers who have the required subject expertise to take time to assist with the withdrawal of materials, so the job is often done poorly or not at all. In many situations, the best advice is to follow guidelines established in other types of libraries. For example, the circulation history might be examined to determine how often and how recently an item has been consulted. Those never used are less likely to be requested in the future. In some libraries, lists are circulated to faculty, lawyers, judges, or whomever the clientele may be. These lists contain titles that have been removed from the active shelves to temporary storage, and people are invited to comment upon or review the books before they are discarded. In a few instances, cooperative retention plans exist. For example, in New York City many firm librarians discard titles after determining that the New York Law Institute will retain them. These cooperative efforts have cropped up all over the country to deal effectively with the proliferation of law materials.

Because of the importance of weeding, it should be considered an integral part of collection development. As with acquisitions, weeding policies should be documented either as part of the collection development policy or on their own. A discard policy, sometimes referred to as a "sunset" policy, may consist of simply one or two sentences indicating that such a procedure is performed. Whether or not a policy is written, it is essential that the librarian set aside time for the withdrawal of outdated materials. In addition to ensuring that much needed space is made available, this policy serves to protect the user from providing inaccurate legal advice to the client.

REFERENCE NOTES

1. Long, R. M.; Martin, H. S.; Buckwalter, R. L. Acquisitions. *In: Law librarianship: a handbook*. Littleton, CO: Rothman; 1983:237.

2. Jacobstein, J. Myron; Mersky, Roy M. *Legal research illustrated*. 1987 ed. Mineola, NY: Foundation Press; 1987:7, 12.

3. Serial trends: legal publishing in the eighties. *Ulrich's News* 2(3):1; 1989.

4. Middleton, Martha. Law reviews get fatter and longer. *National Law Journal* p. 9; 1989 Jan. 9.

5. Scott, Bettie. Price index for legal publications, 1988-89. *Law Library Journal* 82(1):193-196; 1990.

6. Long, R. M.; Martin, H. S; Buckwalter, R. C. Acquisitions. *In: Law librarianship: a handbook*. Littleton, CO: Rothman: 1983:238.

7. American Bar Association. *Approval of law schools; American Bar Association standards and rules of procedure as amended*. Chicago, IL: ABA; 1981.

8. American Association of Law Libraries. Committee on Law Library Service to Prisoners. *Recommended collections for prisons and other institution law libraries*. Rev. ed. Chicago, IL: AALL; 1976.

9. American Correctional Association. *Providing legal services for prisoners: a tool for correctional administrators*. College Park, MD: ACA; 1977.

10. Federal Trade Commission. *Guidelines for the law book industry*. Washington: The Commission; 1975 August 8. Also located at 16 C.F.R. Part 256.

BIBLIOGRAPHY

Campbell, Vivian L. Collection development policy statements: rationales and uses. *Trends in Law Library Management and Technology*. 2(10):1-4; 1989.
　　The author explains why collection development policies are important.
Long, Rosalee M.; Martin, Harry S.; Buckwalter, Robert L. Acquisitions. *In*: Mueller, Heinz P.; Kehoe, Patrick E., eds. *Law librarianship: a handbook*. Littleton, CO: Rothman; 1983:207-328.
　　This chapter identifies the need for collection development policies and includes a number of sample policies. Resources for locating current and retrospective titles for foreign and U.S. materials are also presented.
Serial trends: legal publishing in the eighties. *Ulrich's News*. 2(3):1; 1989.
　　This article reports some alarming statistics regarding the rapid growth in new titles and price increases of legal serials.
Sloane, Richard. Some old and new remedies for thinning law libraries. *New York Law Journal*. 1987 Mar. 17; 4.
　　The author suggests some practical ideas for weeding.
Stoppel, Kaye V. Superseded materials in the law library. *Law Library Journal*. 78(4):465-480; 1986.
　　This article is the result of a survey of how law libraries decide what superseded materials to retain, and whether they are moved to an alternate shelf location.
Weeding the collection: a panel. *Law Library Journal*. 54:389; 1961.
　　This panel discussion, held at the annual AALL meeting, covered the discard and retention policies of law libraries.

Chapter 4

Technical Services

Law libraries, like many special libraries, have traditionally placed more emphasis on reader and reference services than on technical services. However, research capabilities are severely hindered if the technical aspects of librarianship are ignored or de-emphasized. Even today, this attitude remains prevalent in private law libraries of firms, corporations, and bar associations. Fortunately, the librarians in these institutions have benefited from the academic law libraries, where the value of good technical processing has always been recognized and respected. In addition, with the increasing need for cooperation among libraries and the availability of on-line cataloging systems such as OCLC and RLIN, many small and specialized law libraries are recognizing the need for more sophisticated procedures and standardized practices in technical services.

LIBRARY ACQUISITIONS

Once a book has been selected, an order is placed with the publisher or a book jobber. In many instances, this is really only the beginning of the acquisitions process because the majority of law books are either updated regularly (weekly, monthly, annually) or irregularly as the subject matter changes. Law is in a constant state of flux; new bills are introduced in the city, state, and federal legislatures, and new cases that interpret the law are heard in the courts. Agencies and other rule-making bodies regularly consider and put into effect new regulations. Lawyers must, to represent their clients to the best of their ability, always keep abreast of these changes. This means that they cannot rely on a book published even a year or two ago, unless they take steps to ensure that new legal developments have not occurred in that field of law. Law book publishers, responding to the market demand, have developed the process of issuing supplements to lengthen a book's lifetime, thereby increasing its sales and avoiding its obsolescence. These methods of updating place a heavy burden on the librarian to ensure that each book is accurate and current. For simplicity's sake, it would be ideal if law books were all updated once a year, but that is unrealistic. Some fields of law are relatively static, while others are in a period of rapid change. No librarian would be willing to pay for an annual supplement that did not have changes to report, nor would a librarian be willing to wait an entire year for the latest laws to be incorporated.

Standing Order Plans

To ensure that purchased materials are kept up to date, most law librarians establish standing order plans whenever possible. Otherwise, a significant amount of money in original purchase price is wasted because the title is not kept current. Most standing order plans allow the option of returning something if dissatisfied, although there are variations among publishers. The three main types of standing order plans are (1) for supplements to a previously purchased title, (2) for new editions of a previously purchased title, or (3) for all titles published by a publisher or group.

Often, librarians will select the first two options, having determined that the title was worth the original purchase price. Unfortunately, some publishers offer very low original purchase prices, then charge extraordinarily high upkeep costs. Experienced law librarians always inquire about annual upkeep costs before purchasing and are actively working with publishers to develop better scheduling and pricing data for supplements.

Approval Plans

Most publishers will allow librarians to order books on 10- to 30-day approval. This procedure is very useful when brochures are inadequate and librarians are uncertain about a title's quality or relevance to the library's clientele. It is burdensome and costly, however, to record orders, receipt, and return information, and bills can easily be paid by mistake. Therefore, the approval plan is not recommended as a substitute for screening brochures and reviews.

Rush Orders

Like many special libraries, law libraries—especially law firm libraries—must have special procedures in place to handle requests for material needed immediately. Most publishers will accept phone orders and will send titles on an expedited basis, and jobbers and service bureaus may be able to assist in such instances.

Acquisitions Records

The maintenance of acquisitions records in law libraries is essentially the same as in any type of library. The main distinction is, perhaps, that a higher percentage of titles (as many as 90%) will be updated in some fashion. Therefore, acquisitions records are referred to and updated regularly, and are often kept together with a Kardex or check-in system used for recording serials or supplements.

The acquisition record should include a complete listing of author(s), title, publisher (with address and phone number), jobber (if applicable), date of order, the person who authorized the purchase, the person who requested the purchase, the type of transaction (i.e., standing order, 30-day approval, expedited order), and special processing requests to be followed upon receipt (such as "Catalog and send to Mr. Brown ASAP"). Also helpful is expected frequency of supplementation.

CHECK-IN SYSTEMS FOR SERIAL RECORDS

Once an item is received, a check-in system ensures that updates are received and properly processed to "join" the existing materials. Again, the requirements for check-in controls are much like those of the technical services department of any library. However, it is extremely important that library staff regularly check to be certain that all titles are current and complete. A lapsed subscription can be costly to any library, but missing the latest supplement to legal information could result in serious problems for the lawyer and client.

ROUTING

Most law libraries make serial titles available to their clientele. Routing journals serves a dual purpose: to keep clientele abreast of new developments in their fields and to remind them of the library's value as an information resource. In academic institutions, faculty are able to review new journals, law reviews, and other useful material. In law firms, this routing service is usually available to lawyers and paralegals, and in court libraries, to judges and law clerks.

Maintaining accurate records can be a time-consuming and political mess, since establishing seniority lists requires consideration of both power and need, and recipients are constantly changing titles. To intensify the problem, some recipients hoard information, holding items indefinitely, never passing them along to the next person on the list, or returning them to the library for public use. Although libraries recognize the value of circulating such titles, most law librarians would secretly like to banish the practice.

In some law libraries, new issues are not circulated. Instead, the tables of contents are distributed, and articles are provided upon request. Although this practice does ensure that the materials are available to others, it, too, is a time-consuming and costly venture. Librarians must carefully evaluate such programs to be certain that they are in compliance with copyright laws.

MISSING BOOKS

A major problem for libraries worldwide is missing books, and law libraries are equally concerned. In the classic movie "The Paper Chase," competition among law school students was so fierce that they stole, hid, or destroyed library books to keep other students from finding the necessary case or law. In bar and county libraries, it is less common but still a problem. In law firms, where it might not be expected, associates do the bulk of research and are competing with each other for the partner's recognition. Only a small percentage of each associate class will be asked to stay on as partners, and some lawyers will go to great lengths to stand out. Consequently, books are occasionally removed from the library without being signed out, although most do eventually return.

Even more frequent than the intentional hidden volume is the book removed in a hurry "just for a day or two." Lawyers do not stop to consider that a colleague may need the same material. Law libraries are constantly looking for ways to maintain tighter controls, and, at least, maintain records of the missing titles. Determining whether the volume should be replaced is a complex question. Will it eventually be returned? Is it worth the cost of replacement? Is it available elsewhere? Will it simply be lost again? Each law librarian must establish policies and procedures for recording and replacing lost books consistent with the collection development policy.

SUPERSEDED MATERIAL

A major concern of both technical services and reference law librarians is retention policies. Many laws and regulations are promulgated annually by state and federal governments, and many of these laws replace others. Many of the older laws have historical value or may be applicable to certain cases not yet resolved that arose before the law was amended or repealed. It is difficult to determine which materials to retain, and extremely important to distinguish superseded from current legal materials. The technical services division must work closely with the publishers, reference librarians, and lawyers to ensure that superseded titles are clearly identified and separated from the current collection and not inadvertently mistaken for current.

PRESERVATION

Always of concern to academic libraries, and more recently with other types of law libraries, is preservation of historical materials. Although the private law library will probably always rely on the academic and bar libraries for the majority of legal research materials, there is a genuine concern among all librarians that our legal heritage will vanish as books disintegrate. Law libraries are beginning to realize that, along with their other managerial problems, they must focus attention on acid-free paper and methods of salvaging titles that are showing signs of deterioration.

CATALOGING AND CLASSIFICATION

Because law collections were often quite small and manageable, for many years law librarians focused exclusively on what was in the books rather than how to make them more accessible to others. Law books were already logically organized by jurisdiction, many were sequentially numbered sets, and indexing was considered sufficient. Treatises, if organized in any way, were color-coded by broad subject or were simply shelved alphabetically by author or title. Call numbers were nonexistent, as were card catalogs. A simple shelf list was thought adequate.

As libraries, particularly law school libraries, grew, it became necessary to consider more elaborate organizational and indexing schemes to facilitate access. Collections became too large for lawyers to rely on an individual librarian to know the content of the collection, and lawyers wanted to be independent. When the Library of Congress classification scheme for law (Class K) finally became available in 1967, many academic law libraries also adopted these standard classification arrangements and subject headings to enhance cooperative acquisitions and cataloging, thereby reducing operating costs.

Private firm, government, bar, and other law libraries, which tend to be much smaller, have been significantly slower to accept these standardized systems. Because they are smaller, there is more satisfaction with the existing organization and a reluctance to incur conversion costs. Secondly, these smaller collections, which tend to be highly specialized, do not fit as well into a standardized scheme. With easy access to OCLC and RLIN, even these smaller libraries have recognized the value of standardization. LC classification and cataloging, with minor customized treatment, is growing in use among all types of law libraries.

Nonetheless, there are many materials that are not arranged by LC classification. A large part of any law collection is still arranged by type of material, or by jurisdiction, particularly in smaller libraries. Although the arrangement of the collection usually seems perfectly clear to the lawyer or law librarian, acclimation to the collection is difficult for the novice.

Access to most law libraries, except in very small private collections, is enhanced by a card catalog, book catalog, COM (computer output microform) catalog, or on-line catalog. In most libraries, material can be searched by author, title, and subject. Closing the card catalog is gaining in popularity as automated systems improve and become less costly to purchase and use. For example, turn-key systems, once developed for only the largest public and academic libraries, have been developed for smaller, more specialized collections. These PC or mainframe systems are fairly inexpensive, designed for easy implementation and adaptation, and are becoming increasingly common. Because lawyers and law school students are exposed to LEXIS and Westlaw, many law library users readily adapt to the sophisticated search options available with an on-line catalog.

MANAGING SPECIAL COLLECTIONS

Law libraries, which have always maintained vertical files, are faced with growing challenges to provide access to special types of information such as memoranda files, video cassettes, computer databases, and CD-ROMs. Many practices and procedures must be developed in the coming years to capture the information contained in these valuable research materials. Even the small law library must keep abreast of ways to facilitate awareness of these various tools. It is exciting that law librarians have finally left the "Dark Ages" and are adapting to the new formats of information.

BIBLIOGRAPHY

Buchanan, Sally A. Administering the library conservation program. *Law Library Journal*. 77:569-574; 1984-85.
   The author briefly describes the cause for concern and points to consider in establishing an effective conservation and preservation program in a law library.
Evans, Martha M. A history of the development of classification K (law) at the Library of Congress. *Law Library Journal*. 62:25-39; 1969.

The author relates the listing of LC Classification of law materials.

Nainis, Linda et al. Why GPO should use alkaline paper. *DttP (Documents to the People).* 16:38-41; 1988 Mar.

The authors criticize the GPO for using acidic paper in printing valuable historical materials and suggest that if the GPO converted to alkaline paper other
publishers would follow suit.

Norten, Melanie Nietmann; Hirst, Donna. Computerized cataloging in law libraries: OCLC and RLIN compared. *Law Library Journal.* 73:107-128; 1980.

The authors discuss reasons for the slow acceptance of automated cataloging in
law libraries and compare the two major on-line systems.

Ochal, Bethamy J. Microform management: a practical note. *Law Library Journal.* 76:383-385; 1983.

The author presents practical advice for record keeping and storing of microform collections.

Piper, Patricia L.; Kwan, Cecilia H. L. Cataloging and classification practices in
law libraries: update. *Law Library Journal.* 75:375-380; 1982.

The authors describe a 1981 survey in which they determined that law library
cataloging and classification practices were becoming standardized.

Sloane, Richard. A realist's response to illiteracy. *New York Law Journal.* p. 4
col. 1, 1988 Sept. 13.

The author proposes shelving books by color instead of by classifying them!

Stoppel, Kaye V. Superseded material in the Law Library. *Law Library Journal.*
78:465-480; 1986.

The author describes difficulties in determining whether to retain superseded
materials and presents the results of a survey.

Vamberg, Joseph T. The new scope and content of cooperative cataloging for law
libraries. *Law Library Journal.* 60: 244-248; 1967.

The author describes automation projects relating to classification and cataloging in law libraries.

Chapter 5

User Services

INFORMATION NEEDS OF THE CLIENTELE

Lawyers, judges, law school students, and legislators routinely expect librarians to meet their information needs. It could be argued that these are not truly unique demands of lawyers and legal researchers; what makes them unique is that these patrons routinely expect that the research librarians provide will encompass *all* these factors:

1. *Timeliness*: The information requested is usually required immediately. This urgency is real; the lawyer may need to read, analyze, and form an argument in the same day. In many law libraries, librarians do not bother to ask when an answer is required, since it is understood that it is a rush. In others, they ask patrons to define "rush" or "ASAP" as same *day* or same *hour*.

2. *Currency*: "I need up-to-the-minute status on . . ." is frequently heard in legislative libraries or in law libraries where patrons include lobbyists. It is also required by lawyers on their way to court. Many cases are based on precedent; that is, how the courts resolved similar cases in the past. If a lawyer bases his argument on case X, he must know with certainty that case X was not appealed or, even worse, overturned, by a higher court. Last year's (or last week's) statute is also unacceptable. Arguing a case using outdated laws is not only embarrassing but could be critical to the outcome of the case or could result in a malpractice claim. Therefore, it is crucial that lawyers keep abreast of daily legal developments.

3. *Accuracy*: Every library patron should be given the correct information, but studies show that is not the reality. Librarians should be doubly cautious in providing correct information to law-

yers, since it is conceivable that a wrong answer could result in a client's financial or personal ruin.

4. *Thoroughness*: The information provided should be the culmination of a complete and thorough search. In few instances are librarians told much about the reason for needing the information, and they certainly should not make decisions about what the patron really needs. The lawyer should be given all requested materials, and every effort should be made to address all avenues.

5. *Detail*: The lawyer is often concerned not only with the wording of a statute or contract but also with the wording of newspaper articles, advertisements, government statistics, and other textual material. Because lawyers are in the business of presenting the facts of a case to prove their point, librarians may be sent on missions to locate data worded in a particular way.

6. *Format*: Lawyers often want to see an answer in a chart, graph, or statistical table. While every effort should be made to accommodate the lawyer, librarians must not disregard information found in another format. The lawyer should know that the alternatively formatted data may be more current or may contradict the requested chart or table. Usually the librarian should not compile the chart or table but should only provide source materials. If this is not the case, it is extremely important to keep primary documents and attach them or carefully cite them.

Another request librarians receive is to provide an original document or a copy of it. When possible, any documents used as evidence should be provided in their original rather than in an electronic or microform version. Although the courts will accept these equivalents when necessary, they prefer the original or a standard photocopy. It is often not the whim of the lawyer but the rules of the court that are responsible for these format demands.

7. *Absolute Need*: Law librarians have all heard "I must have it; it must exist" and will laugh at memories of such statements, but few librarians laughed at the time of the request. Lawyers do not accept "no" for an answer. If the request is difficult, every source consulted should be recorded. Before giving up, every written and on-line source should be exhausted, then the librarian should contact other librarians to brainstorm. Checking the *Encyclopedia of Associations* and either calling associations' libraries or resource

centers or providing the patron with those telephone numbers is the next step. Law librarians frequently attempt to locate government experts, since they exist for almost everything. However, such calls should be made only after receiving clearance from the person who initiated the research. (See the section on confidentiality, No. 10.) Only after all written, on-line, and telephone/people resources have been exhausted and recorded should the law librarian admit defeat.

8. *"The Next Best Thing"*: Once the librarian has determined that the specific answer does not exist, creativity is required to find something similar. Lawyers do this automatically and expect librarians to do so also. If the librarian cannot find any cases about chimpanzees, he or she should look for some on orangutans. Trying to broaden or narrow the scope or substituting one thing for another becomes part of the reference process.

9. *Never Say Never, and Never Say No*: Something has been written on everything, and giving something related or limited in scope is better than giving nothing at all. A 1961 thesis may be the only thing the librarian can find, but it is probably better than nothing. In any case, it is not a determination for the librarian to make; he or she should give everything available. Similarly, there are always limits to librarians' abilities and time. Librarians should always do *something*: if the question is not understood, asking for an explanation or looking up terms in a law dictionary is required. If the library does not have the resources (collection or staffing, for example), the librarian should provide names and telephone numbers or bibliographies to help the patron find the answer elsewhere.

10. *Confidentiality*: All questions should be treated confidentially. Librarians must never talk about requests outside of the library, and even internally, they must keep the talk quiet and restrict it to those who need to know. Librarians must *never* call outside sources, even other libraries, until they have been authorized to do so. Many individual client matters are private and personal, and many corporate matters are secret as well. Since the librarian rarely knows full details of lawyers' cases, all requests should be held in the strictest confidence.

11. *Non-legal Research*: Many lawyers who formerly researched only the traditional legal materials are now taking an interdisciplinary approach to their research. Legal research centers today are

relying more and more on nonlegal research tools. In addition to locating laws, regulations, and cases, librarians are asked for emergency room procedures, information on the transport of environmental pollutants, market share of companies, and endless other facts. Law librarians are even asked for fiction, since many lawyers quote from the classics in their closing arguments.

12. *Limitations*: As non-lawyers, librarians must be aware of their limitations. There is a fine line between doing legal research and doing factual research, but librarians should be careful not to cross that line. The librarian has a responsibility to provide current, complete, and accurate research, but they should not go beyond that into interpretation unless they possess the JD and the firm's support.

LEGAL DATABASES

The methods of legal research began to change during the 1970s and, even more so, in the 1980s, with the availability and expansion of "CALR," or Computer-Assisted Legal Research. The first publicly available legal database was LEXIS, originally called OBAR. It was developed in the late 1960s by the Ohio State Bar Association and Data Corporation of Dayton, Ohio, to meet the needs of its members. In 1970, Data Corporation merged into the Mead Corporation to become a subsidiary, Mead Data Central. The database originally consisted of Ohio State materials but expanded rapidly to include other state and federal material. When it was first marketed nationally in the early 1970s, resistance was quite high. Lawyers listed among their concerns typographical errors and errors of omission, misinformation regarding the content of the database, and security issues. Reluctantly, large law firms signed on with the system on a trial basis, only to learn there were, indeed, many benefits to CALR. Usage began to grow, and LEXIS was asked to add more cases to the system, and to add additional search capabilities.

West Publishing Company, the leading case reporting publisher in the United States, watched closely as the LEXIS following spread throughout the legal community. Although originally opposed to entering a different line of business, West eventually realized that it was necessary to compete with LEXIS to retain its loyal clientele, and in 1975 Westlaw was born.

Today, these two systems are the major legal research databases of their kind. Acceptance is so wide "Lawyers who do not know what LEXIS and Westlaw offer are practicing law with blinders. They will suffer what they deserve."[1] Each of the systems offers a wide variety of legal databases, with slightly different contents, search capabilities, and pricing. Veralex, a joint venture between Mead Data and Lawyers' Cooperative Publishing Company, is a case retrieval system that allows a user to enter a citation and retrieve the full text of the case, but free-text searching is not available. In addition, there are one or two noncommercial legal databases, such as JURIS, created by the Department of Justice. Although LEXIS has a larger share of the market, that share has been decreasing slowly during the last five years as Westlaw has been marketed more aggressively. Competition between the two vendors is fierce, and there have been several law suits between Mead Data Central and West Publishing Company.

Today lawyers often have access to one or both on-line systems. The benefits of wide availability of LEXIS and Westlaw are many. First, even solo practitioners now have access to millions of cases without having to purchase or house the equivalent expensive sets of books. This has also benefited large firm, academic, and government law libraries where space and budget constraints have resulted in stricter limits on owning printed sets. Lawyers who might have had access only to their own state's material are now able to access cases and related materials nationwide. Both LEXIS and Westlaw also make available decisions never reported in any printed casebooks. Decisions are made available in a very timely way, with most Supreme Court cases searchable within 24 hours. And finally, both LEXIS and Westlaw are continuously enhancing their systems with the full text of federal and state laws, regulations, and other legal research resources. Consequently, access to a wide variety of legal research tools is available at relatively low cost. On-line access provides an invaluable resource to lawyers regardless of space or budget problems.

There are several reasons to use on-line systems even if the printed version is readily available. For example, an on-line search is often much faster than traditional book research. CALR also enables the researcher to combine terms or search for words or phrases not found in indexes. This saves hours of cross-indexing or may locate cases with peculiar circumstances which could never be retrieved through traditional research.

Despite all the positive aspects of computerized legal research, there are some strong drawbacks as well. As previously stated, the database vendors are constantly updating and improving their contents and search capabilities, making it difficult for end-users to remain abreast of the new developments. The teaching of computer-assisted legal research should be an ongoing procedure rather than the one-time event that it generally is. Although vendors do attempt to educate end-users by offering free refresher courses, special newsletters, announcements, and on-line help features, too few lawyers recognize the need or make time for advanced training.

Another problem is that the vendors of LEXIS and Westlaw have been so effective in marketing their products that lawyers have begun to rely too heavily on CALR to the exclusion of traditional resources. On the rare occasions when the systems are unavailable (during power outages, for example), a growing number of lawyers are unable to continue their research using the books. They are simply unfamiliar with the digests, encyclopedias, and other types of traditional print resources.

Related to this problem is the fact that when lawyers do not locate what they need from LEXIS and Westlaw, they assume that the material does not exist. Many lawyers do not recognize that these databases, while massive, do not contain everything. Lawyers also assume that LEXIS and Westlaw are always more current than their printed equivalent. Although this is usually true, there are occasions when a loose-leaf service, advance sheet, or other paper product contains more current laws, regulations, or cases.

As with any on-line system, there are errors in the databases. Both LEXIS and Westlaw are generally very high quality, but there are typographical errors, errors of omission, and, on rare occasions, more significant errors. It is possible to miss an important case or other document because of an error in the system.

More likely, of course, is a search mistake. Many lawyers, busy with the practice of law, do not search effectively or efficiently.

Synonyms may not be used, variant spellings may be overlooked, or the lawyer may be searching the wrong file or using syntax incorrectly. It is not hard to imagine the number of errors made by end-users when professional librarians experience frustration about keeping up their own expert searching skills.

Finally, lawyers sometimes overlook the cost of the databases. Law schools are often provided with free access to LEXIS and Westlaw for teaching purposes. When students graduate and begin their professional practice, they have no concept of the expense involved in performing on-line searches. The first bill from the vendor is sometimes a tremendous shock. While private practitioners often pass such charges on to the client, it is not always possible to do so, especially with today's client inspecting and challenging escalating legal fees.

LEGISLATIVE DATABASES

In addition to LEXIS and Westlaw, there are several legislative databases in use today. Because they each use different search language and contain different information, these are used primarily by specialists, such as librarians, legislative researchers, or paralegals. Rarely are they used directly by lawyers. The most commonly known systems are LEGI-SLATE and CCH ELSS. In New York State, LRS (Legislative Retrieval System) is available.

NON-LEGAL DATABASES

Although LEXIS and Westlaw are the primary databases used by lawyers, there is a growing interest in non-legal research tools. Lawyers in all areas must access non-legal information in order to represent clients. Litigators, for example, must become overnight experts in medicine, engineering, or an industry. Labor lawyers must keep abreast of employment-related issues, such as day care trends, AIDS and other health conditions, and employee stock option agreements. To learn about non-legal fields, lawyers are turning to non-legal databases such as NEXIS, DIALOG, Dow Jones, Vutext, Datatimes, and BRS. Fortunately, the vast majority of lawyers have recognized that they must rely on a librarian to identify the best resources and perform these database searches.

REFERENCE NOTE

1. Harrington, William G. Use of LEXIS, and Westlaw too, is vital to any law practice. *National Law Journal*. p. 18, 20; 1987 Oct. 12.

BIBLIOGRAPHY

Berring, Robert C. Editorial. *Legal Reference Services Quarterly*. 7(1):1-2; 1987 Spring.
 Berring argues that most of what legal reference librarians provide is legal reference rather than legal research. His admittedly unpopular view calls for increased emphasis on ready reference skills.
Bing, Jon. Performance of legal text retrieval systems: the curse of Boole. *Law Library Journal*. 79:187-202; 1987.
 This article continued the great debate on the pros and cons of on-line searching in legal databases.
Brecht, Albert. Changes in legal scholarship and their impact on law school library reference services. *Law Library Journal*. 77:157-164; 1984-85.
 The author describes the increasing emphasis on interdisciplinary legal research and the resulting added demands on legal reference libraries.
Coco, Al. Full text revisited. *Legal Reference Services Quarterly*. 6(3/4):195-197; 1986 Fall/Winter.
 The author advises adding editorial components to full-text systems to enhance them.
Dabney, Daniel P. The Curse of Thamus: an analysis of full-text legal document retrieval. *Law Library Journal*. 78(1):5-40; 1986.
 The author discusses the pitfalls of full-text legal document searching of large CALR systems, and sparked a flurry of debate.
Danner, Richard A. Reference theory and the future of legal reference service. *Law Library Journal*. 76:217-232; 1983.
 The author applies reference theory to law libraries and discusses the impact automated legal research and full-text database access will have on the law librarian.
_____. From the editor: working with facts. *Law Library Journal*. 79:611-616; 1987.
 This editorial discusses the need for improved understanding of legal research methods and of the new guides available to help teach students.
Griffith, Cary. Dual-system research: the best of both worlds. *Legal Times*. p. 9-10. 1986 March 17.

The author advises that anyone using computer-assisted legal research subscribe to both LEXIS and Westlaw rather than relying entirely on either one.

Griffith, Cary. Cost effective computer-assisted legal research, or when two are better than one. *Legal Reference Services Quarterly*. 7(1):3-13; 1987 Spring.
The author advocates use of both LEXIS and Westlaw.

Harrington, William G. A brief history of computer-assisted legal research. *Law Library Journal*. 77:543-556; 1984-85.
The author, one of the founding fathers of on-line legal research, presents an interesting history of computer-assisted legal research.

Harrington, William G. Use of LEXIS, and Westlaw too, is vital to any law practice. *National Law Journal*. p. 18, 20; 1987 Oct. 12.
This article, written by a practising lawyer, advises that lawyers who think they can practice law today without LEXIS or Westlaw take another look.

Harrington, William G.; Wilson, H. Donald; Bennett, Robert L. The Mead Data Central system of computerized legal research. *Law Library Journal*. 64:184-189; 1971.
The authors present a brief history and the basic features of LEXIS in its early years.

Laskowitz, Roberta. Roberta's rules of reference. *In*: Wallace and Wrenn, co-chairpersons, *Private law librarians, 1986*. New York, NY: Practising Law Institute; 1986:19-30.
This chapter, presented at an all-day seminar for law librarians, is in expanded outline format. Nonetheless, reviewing these rules is an excellent way to learn quickly how law librarians' skills must be applied to perform legal research effectively.

Mills, Robin K. Reference service vs. legal advice: is it possible to draw the line? *Law Library Journal*. 72:179-193; 1979.
The author provides several examples of questions that border on legal advice versus legal reference.

Reader service in law libraries. *Law Library Journal*. 64:486-506; 1971.
Four panelists discuss bibliographic tools, automation, and circulation in law libraries at the 1971 AALL annual meeting.

Rosenberg, John. Commentary: let legal researcher beware: on-line tricks, traps, tips. *Legal Times*. p.11; 1987 April 13.
The author explains flaws of database searching and design and advises caution when using on-line systems.

Stephens, Joe K. LEXIS vs Westlaw: the contest heats up. *Legal Administrator*. p. 42-48. 1987 Sep./Oct.
The author compares LEXIS and Westlaw and concludes that the preferred data base depends upon which factors the user finds most important.

Tormey, Mary Jo, moderator. Legal reference service: the delivery process. *Law Library Journal*. 77:47-64; 1979 Winter.
This article is actually a panel discussion presented by the Michigan Association of Law Libraries in 1978. Topics covered were: the reference communication process, the problem patron, and the unauthorized practice of law.

Warnken, Kelly. A study in LEXIS and Westlaw errors. *Legal Economics*. p. 39, 58; 1987 July/August.

This article reports the results of a 1983-84 study comparing LEXIS and Westlaw. The author concludes that each system contained errors but both are still worthwhile research tools.

Woxland, Tom. A day in the life of a law school reference librarian. *Legal Reference Services Quarterly*. 7(1):111-113; 1987 Spring.

This brief article takes a humorous look at the questions a legal reference librarian is expected to answer in a day's work.

Chapter 6

The Impact of Technology on Law Libraries

With the proliferation of the written word affecting every type of library and business, it is not surprising that law libraries are under growing pressure to explore new technological developments that have the potential to solve or lessen space and budget constraints.

MICROFILM AND MICROFICHE

One of the first advances seen in law libraries was microfilm and microfiche. Although these materials were expensive to purchase and had to be stored under special environmental conditions, they did offer an alternative to standard printed works. Microformat offered significant space savings or availability of material formerly accessed through interlibrary loan. It was accepted with some reluctance, however, for several reasons. First, the library needed to buy equipment to read and print back the film or fiche. Equipment is expensive to maintain and service. Printouts, although much improved thanks to today's high-quality machines, are rarely as easy to read as a standard photocopy. End-users remain reluctant to use the equipment, so staff must assist users or provide the printing service. Storage needs are complex, also. Specially built cabinets are required, floor weight loads may need reinforcement, and temperature and humidity levels must be controlled. Even using an elastic band around a roll of microfilm can damage the film. Microfiche, widely preferred over film, has been problematic in that a card is easily misfiled, lost, or even stolen. Law librarians were pleased as other options became available, although many libraries have already invested in major collections of microfilm and fiche.

COMPUTER DATABASES

As discussed in the previous chapter, the initial fear and reluctance toward LEXIS, Westlaw, and other databases was soon replaced by overwhelming praise. Shock waves over the exorbitant searching costs, however, are still common today. Locating and printing a single case almost always costs more than $25, with printing alone costing 2¢ per line. Although this is certainly preferable to a case's unavailability, it is by no means a replacement for the books. Most law librarians advocate the use of LEXIS and Westlaw as research aids to supplement rather than replace the printed sources. It is advisable to perform a search, print out citations, and sign off. Lawyers are usually discouraged from reading cases from the screen (although reading on-line is uncomfortable anyway) or from printing the full text of decisions or other materials on-line. Unfortunately, educating lawyers about the high cost is a growing problem for librarians as access to these systems is made easier. Not many years ago, lawyers were required to sit at a designated terminal to use LEXIS or Westlaw. Librarians could then easily monitor use and offer advice and training. Today, lawyers often have access in their offices and at home via a personal computer, making it nearly impossible for the librarian to intervene.

Even non-legal databases are growing in popularity among lawyers, and librarians will encounter growing problems with end-user searching.

CD-ROMS

A relative newcomer to law libraries is CD-ROM technology. Early in 1989, West Publishing Company announced the availability of several CD-ROM products, and several other vendors have been marketing products since 1987. While no one yet knows how such products will affect law libraries of the future, most librarians expect that, like databases, these disks will supplement rather than replace books. Indeed, it is likely that they will compete more directly with the databases than the books because of their price structure. CD-ROMs, although expensive to purchase, do offer the distinct advantage of no search or connect charges. This feature is attractive to librarians because it allows them to budget more accurately. Also, end-users can be encouraged to try various search strategies and to use the system freely without fear of generating exorbitant on-line costs.

One major drawback of CD-ROMs is the lack of standards. As more vendors enter the marketplace, law librarians may be forced into buying hardware and software packages unique to each product. This will be expensive, require more space, and increase the confusion regarding when and how to choose a particular type of research tool.

Audio-cassettes, although available from several vendors, never attracted much attention from lawyers or law school students. Cassettes that are most common in law libraries are recordings of continuing legal education seminars and the occasional current awareness service on tape.

Videotapes, on the other hand, have attracted far more attention. Law schools and law firms have collected a variety of in-house and commercially-produced videotapes to enhance their library collections. Particularly in law schools, videotapes are used heavily for classroom teaching or made available to students to supplement their research. In law firms, purchasing the videotape is a cost-effective way to provide continuing education to many lawyers without requiring travel or allowing schedule conflicts to interfere.

Interactive video has also made its way into the law schools. Interactive videodisk programs combine the computer with the videodisk. This technology was first used to teach doctors how to respond to medical problems in emergency rooms but has recently found acceptance among the legal community. These programs are used to teach or enhance the teaching of legal research or trial practice skills by simulating real-life situations. Most often, the lessons are mock trials in which the student acts as counsel and uses the keyboard to raise objections. Once an objection is raised, the computer "judge" asks the user to cite grounds for the objection. If the judge rules in favor of the objection, the trial continues. If the judge overrules, the system provides an explanation. If the student misses an opportunity to object, the oversight is reviewed at the end of the program. Most often found in law schools, these interactive video programs are beginning to make their way into law firms. Some lawyers complain, however, that the system is too much like a video game with programmed by-the-book objections which, in some cases, are better left unraised. The hardware required costs as little as $1,000. Most run on an IBM PC with color monitor and a laser disk player.

Law librarians need to keep these valuable options in mind when providing research tools to lawyers. In addition, they must consider storage requirements, equipment needs, and viewing and lending policies and practices.

THE LIBRARIAN AS CONSUMER

The law librarian must increasingly become an educated consumer to make intelligent purchasing decisions. Law librarians must be sophisticated in their knowledge of both traditional legal research tools and the new techniques. They must be able to compare and contrast one against the other in purchase costs, use costs, contents, search capabilities and commands, accuracy, and currency. They must be able to evaluate space and environmental requirements, evaluate hardware and software, read contracts, and make sound business decisions. The choices facing law librarians may have long-lasting consequences in terms of how legal research is performed in the future.

THE LIBRARIAN AS EDUCATOR

The librarian's responsibility does not end with purchasing decisions. Given the complexity of the legal system in the United States and the growing interest in legal systems worldwide, law schools today must emphasize the teaching of the theoretical and conceptual framework of law rather than the programmed legal research tools and techniques. The law library profession, therefore, is already experiencing an increased responsibility to teach legal research skills to law students and lawyers. Although law schools require students to take a course in legal research, the general consensus among law librarians and practicing lawyers is that the system is failing. Among the many criticisms are that the courses are taught too early in law school, that they are not given the same weight as other courses, or that they attempt to cover too much ground. Although all these factors may exist, it is also true that the proliferation of legal cases, treatises, on-line research tools, and now CD-ROMs must also be a cause for lawyers' limited research skills. Whatever the causes, the result is that law librarians in all types of libraries will be called upon more often to teach legal research skills. Unfortunately, lawyers may be reluctant students — too busy or unaware of their deficiencies. This will require that law librarians force-feed information through effective marketing, improved documentation, and attractive short classes.

BIBLIOGRAPHY

Bayer, Barry D.; Welch, Mark J. CD technology changing data management. *Connecticut Law Tribune*. 14(28):13; 1988 July 18.
   This article describes what CD-ROMs are, how they can be used in the legal environment, and lists CD-ROM products available in 1988.
Horne, William. The law firm library of the future. *American Lawyer*. Special Pull-Out Section; 1988 Dec.
   This article identifies the technological advances and the managerial questions law librarians face because of them. Emphasis is on the private law firm librarian, many of whom are interviewed.
Kauffman, S. Blair. The future of libraries in a high-tech society: are law books (and libraries) becoming obsolete? *Legal Information Alert*. 7(1):1-3,12; 1988 Jan.
   According to the author, the law librarian's role will increase as technology develops. The book will remain, although collections will be supplemented and made more manageable by technology development.
Law library of the year 2000: [a memo] to the partners from head librarians. *American Lawyer*. Pull-out Management Report; 1989 Dec.
   Six law firm librarians discuss their visions of the law library in the year 2000. All predict an increased role for library staff, with technology having an impact on virtually every aspect of how the library operates.
Miller, Ellen J. Fusion of computer and video creates novel learning tool, develops practical legal skills. *National Law Journal*. Special Section; 1986 Mar. 25; p. 15.
   This article discusses the technology of interactive video and describes some programs in use and under development.

Miller, Ellen J. Interactive video for CLE for lawyers in Florida program starts in fall. *National Law Journal*. 1988 Aug. 29; 17.

The author discusses the pros and cons of using interactive video and describes a program under development in Florida.

Mitchel, Steven E. In print vs. on-line: the paperless law library. *Legal Information Alert*. 7(10):1-3; 1988 Nov.-Dec.

The author explains why the paperless law library is unlikely.

Oliver, Myrna. Video replacing paper chase? *Los Angeles Times*. Metro. Part 2, p. 3 col. 1, 1988 Jan. 16.

Article discusses the development of interactive videodisk technology and its use in law schools.

Reese, Jean; Steffey, Ramona J. The seven deadly sins of CD-ROM. *Laserdisk Professional*. 1988 July:19-24.

The authors discuss the problems with CD-ROMs: hardware and software, space needs, training problems, scheduling and security concerns, hidden costs, and licensing restrictions.

Stone, Dennis J. Institute on emerging technologies asks tough questions of attendees, January 9-12, 1989. *Trends in Law Library Management and Technology*. 2(5):1-3; 1988-1989 Dec.-Jan.

The author presents highlights of the AALL winter institute.

Strain, Laura M. CD-ROM in the private law library: a primer of readings. *In: Managing the private law library 1988*. Co-chaired by Sharon K. French and Susanne Gehringer. New York: Practising Law Institute; 1988: 153-224.

The author collected and reprinted many informative articles on CD-ROMs for distribution at this seminar.

Taylor, Betty W.; Mann, Elizabeth B.; Munro, Robert J. *The twenty-first century: technology's impact on academic research and libraries*. Boston, MA: G. K. Hall, 1988.

The authors forecast the law library of the 21st century, and attempt to lead practicing librarians in the right direction.

Chapter 7

Management Issues

THE LAW LIBRARY DIRECTOR
AND THE ORGANIZATION'S ADMINISTRATION

Few law libraries exist without dependence upon a larger organization or institution. Therefore, the law library director must actively seek the support of administrators of the parent organization to ensure that the library holds a secure and valued position. In academic law libraries, this is slightly easier because of accreditation and professional standards which establish minimum requirements. However, even in such environments, there is growing pressure to contain or reduce costs, and law librarians in all types of organizations must be prepared to justify collection and staffing costs.

The first objective of a law library director should be to review the firm's or university's organizational chart and to secure a strong position within that structure. The librarian should always know which administrators are friends and foes and should strive to gain acceptance and respect in both groups. This acceptance can be accomplished in several subtle and obvious ways, in the form of behavior and with documentation. As managers in other fields have long known, simply being well regarded by their immediate supervisors is no assurance that they or their departments are safe and secure. The library manager must attempt to identify and meet the needs of every administrator. This can be a difficult challenge, since staffing and budget are often limited, and the primary users of the library are most often the students or new lawyers.

Attendance at administrative meetings and functions is mandatory, and these meetings should be viewed as opportunities to impress colleagues and to market the library. Like managers everywhere, librarians should emulate the next level of management in dress and behavior. All too often, librarians dismiss these factors as irrelevant, but like it or not, people are evaluated in part on the basis of their professional appearance and demeanor. Librarians may need to ask to be included and should be prepared to offer valid reasons for attending administrative meetings. They should volunteer to serve on committees and to perform research to assist committees with their work. Law librarians must be acutely aware of the changing needs of the organization and should be innovators who are creative and aggressive in helping the organization meet its goals.

Finally, law library administrators must recognize both those with authority and those with power in the organization. Those with authority (i.e., those holding the titles) may not be the same as those who hold the power. Politics and personal relationships may provide a seemingly inconsequential individual with power to influence the organization.

Documentation can help the library maintain or improve its position within the organization as well. All documents, from the one-page memo to the annual report, should be carefully written and professionally presented. It is a simple fact of life that the typewritten or word-processed document is granted more official status and recognition than a hand-written masterpiece. Among the documents that law librarians should produce are formal goals and objectives, an annual report, a guide to the library, library newsletters, pathfinders, and announcements. Many of these documents, when well prepared, get far wider circulation than might be expected and are usually reviewed by top management.

Although excellent service is among the best ways to secure support, it is also advisable to maintain a variety of statistics. Statistics, while burdensome to compile, provide one of the few quantitative analyses of law libraries. They can play an important role in annual reports, increased staffing requests, and similar situations. The value and type of statistics that should be kept will vary from one law library to the next, but among the numbers to be considered are reference statistics, interlibrary loan statistics, circulation statistics, missing book statistics, and, in law firms, billing statistics.

SPACE PLANNING AND DESIGN

There are many articles and books available today to assist law librarians in planning, designing, and moving law libraries. Unfortunately, all vary somewhat in their advice, making it difficult to determine the best approach. The varying philosophies and recommendations are due in large part to the variety of law libraries. Private firm libraries, for example, generally have very different needs from academic law libraries. However, even within a particular type of law library group, many of the planning decisions must be made within the context of the goals and objectives of the individual organization. Each has defined priorities and peculiarities unique to the organization, and these must be factors in any plans.

Nonetheless, there are several factors common to all law libraries. Virtually every law library is faced with space problems. The avalanche of written legal material has created a burden on law libraries of every size and type. Despite tightened collection development policies, shared acquisitions, aggressive weeding, and conversion to microformats, law libraries are plagued by bursting shelves. It is not unusual for a law library to grow as much as 10% per year.

Secondly, although technology has played a very minor part in reducing space requirements to date, no one really knows what advanced technology will bring. For example, microfilm and microfiche resulted in small space savings for some libraries, but equipment and storage requirements offset most of the savings. In addition, many of the materials converted to film or fiche were secondary materials that might have been eliminated instead. Although LEXIS and Westlaw were originally expected to help combat law library space problems, it rapidly became evident that cost constraints negated that promise. CD-ROMs, the latest technological development, are now predicted to be accepted in law firms as supplements to books rather than as replacements for them, at least for the next five to ten years. Rather than reducing space needs, then, law libraries must add space in which to place additional legal materials such as CD-ROMs and video equipment.

DISASTER PLANNING

Many libraries do not have written disaster plans. Developing a plan is very expensive and time consuming, and is quite a burden given the low odds of an actual disaster occurring. However, a catastrophe is certainly even more disastrous if there are no existing plans to manage one. Disaster preparations should be a part of every law library manager's responsibility.

Types of Disasters

Disasters in libraries are most often associated with fires and floods. Water damage is the most common result of any catastrophe, with smoke and fire damage next. Water damage can result from fires, floods, broken water pipes, or leaky roofs.

Another type of disaster in law libraries is theft or mutilation of materials, although this is far less common than smoke, fire, or water damage.

A fairly new area of concern in law libraries, however, is theft of or damage to computer equipment. There is growing awareness of the need for prevention and disaster planning for hardware and software.

Record Keeping

Law libraries today are often equipped with inventory tools such as the card catalog, shelf list, and serials holding lists. If these are in printed format, it is recommended that a copy is maintained off the premises in case of a disaster. Many law libraries use RLIN or OCLC or other computerized cataloging systems, which usually have the valuable side benefit of the availability of computer tapes of current holdings.

Law libraries would be wise, however, to maintain copies of such records as routing lists, payment ledgers, and other major records that could take weeks or months to replicate otherwise. An inventory of furniture and equipment, including computer hardware and software, should also be maintained off-site. Valuable artwork should be included in this list.

Finally, any special collection, such as memoranda of law or precedents volumes, should be regularly inventoried. Serious consideration should be given to maintaining a duplicate set of all such documents, as these cannot be replaced at any cost. If the private law firm librarian is responsible for such areas as conflicts of interests, these files, too, should be duplicated and maintained off-site.

The Disaster Plan

The disaster plan should be both brief and comprehensive. It must be concise and to the point while covering all aspects of disaster prevention and preparedness. It should include:

1. Library floor plans, including engineering plans and blueprints that show water pipes, sprinklers, shut-off valves, and emergency equipment such as fire extinguishers.
2. Library collection lay-out, so key areas can quickly be identified as most important to save, and later, for identifying losses.
3. Emergency names and telephone numbers of key personnel, such as the librarians, administrators, partners or faculty, and the numbers of fire, police, and other emergency personnel. It is also recommended that numbers of disaster recovery experts be included here to save having to locate them later. The name of the insurance company and agent should also be listed.
4. Procedures to follow in the event of an emergency, including who is in charge overall and who is in charge of various aspects, such as gathering emergency supplies, should be discussed. All members of the disaster team should be identified, including who will handle internal and external communications.
5. Salvage efforts to follow in an emergency should be included. How to sort by degree of damage, how to maintain an inventory of the damaged materials, and how to pack damaged materials should be included.
6. Collection priorities should be identified. The most valuable or irreplaceable items in the collection should be salvaged first, and this material should be pointed out in the manual so the disaster team recognizes its importance.

Valuation

An inventory of materials damaged or destroyed is essential to any insurance claim. As previously stated, the law librarian must be certain to maintain a shelf list and other inventory records in a safe location off-site.

Once the damaged books or other media are identified, the degree of damage must be assessed. Restoration of titles should be carefully considered. Careful cost analysis must be undertaken to determine whether to restore or replace damaged articles. In addition, careful consideration should be given to neither replacing nor restoring the material. It may be wise to determine its usefulness and ready availability elsewhere before investing any money in it. Insurance rarely compensates 100% of the loss, so some judgments should be made as to what is no longer necessary.

To determine replacement costs, publishers' and book dealers' catalogs can be consulted. Rather than determining individual prices on a large periodical or looseleaf collection, it may be wise to estimate the value of the entire collection using published price indices. In any valuation effort, the cost of acquisition, cataloging, and processing should all be calculated when determining replacement costs.

Insurance

All libraries should have adequate insurance coverage, since the cost of rebuilding the collection alone is enormous. Conferring with an insurance consultant is an excellent way to obtain the ideal coverage for the needs of a particular library. Policies vary, and should be analyzed thoroughly to make certain that the insurance plan will provide adequate protection against loss.

Prevention

Law librarians should not neglect the major aspect of disaster planning—prevention. A careful examination of the location of the library with regard to risks of water damage, for example, is a relatively simple task. Identifying possible sources for water leaks may not result in moving the library or relocating pipes, but it can alert the librarian to areas to inspect regularly. Keeping materials away from windowsills or other common areas for water seepage is also advisable.

Instituting a no-smoking policy is another preventive measure. A periodic inspection of wiring in all library areas can reduce electrical fire hazards.

Having a security guard who walks through the library regularly, inspecting for unusual patrons as well as fire and safety hazards, may be advisable.

With careful prevention and planning procedures in place, the disaster will certainly be less catastrophic.

MARKETING THE LAW LIBRARY

Because of growing financial constraints and related reduction of collections and staff, there has been much emphasis recently on marketing the law library. In most special libraries staffing is barely adequate. Overtime work is often standard fare or jobs go undone. Because of time pressures, some librarians will respond to marketing enthusiasts by saying they do not have time to do bill paying or shelving tasks, let alone any marketing of services. Others say they are already well-used and could not handle additional demands. However, a library's heavy use does not mean that it is well-respected or recognized by those who control the budget. Most often, the library users are law school students or new associates with little or no authority over library budget and administration. Therefore, librarians must establish an aggressive marketing plan which will be visible to the partners, faculty, or administrators who have control over space planning, budgeting, staff allocations, and general library management. Because these people may never set foot in the library or take direct advantage of the library resources, aggressive marketing is essential. Word of mouth is obviously very important, but students' and associates' support may not be sufficient to carry the library in a budget crunch.

Ideally, a marketing plan begins with an analysis of present users, nonusers, collection use, hours of peak use, and other demographic and use patterns. However, with a minimum of effort, even the most burdened staff can adopt a "bare bones" approach to marketing with the use of promotional tools, several of which are reviewed below.

The Library Newsletter

There are several well-established methods of marketing the library to non-users. The most frequently cited is the library bulletin or newsletter. Unfortunately, many librarians pay little attention to its potential, simply distributing a list of acquisitions in alphabetical or chronological order. Far too many librarians send out sloppy lists, with typographical errors and handwritten notes. To add value, librarians should make the list easy to browse through and should arrange the titles by subject so readers can scan the contents for their own practice areas.

Although some libraries make use of amateur graphics, these are not recommended because they diminish the professional impact. The intended audience is too sophisticated and will not be amused to see elementary graphics. Law librarians should avoid artwork completely unless it has relevance to the subject matter and keep everything neat and in physical proportion. If graphics are used, they should be smaller than the text so they do not overshadow it.

Another possible inclusion is book reviews of the most notable titles from the new acquisitions list. Having a standard "New & Notable" column with two to ten new titles described in a few sentences may attract the person who cannot be bothered scanning a whole list. It may also bring users to the library to see the book and may remind them that the library recognizes and responds to their needs.

Many law libraries also distribute photocopies of the tables of contents pages of law reviews and legal publications. This reasonably simple practice serves to inform patrons of what is new in the collection. In some cases, the library may also be able to stop paying for subscriptions for individuals who can rely instead on requesting titles they would like the library to send them.

Yet another feature is a continuing legal education calendar, listing dates, sponsors, and titles of seminars. Ideally, as with new acquisitions, seminars are listed by topic for the best reference value.

If the time or staff can possibly be spared, very brief explanations of frequently used topics such as the Standard Industrial Classification codes, the Consumer Price Index, LIBOR (London Interbank Offered Rates), or the General Agreement on Tariffs and Trade are well received by many library users. Explanations of less than one page are recommended, followed by a brief bibliography of resource materials. These feature articles rarely take more than a few hours to prepare and are very often clipped and saved for reference and referral. A by-product is that librarians often learn in the process of writing these articles.

A database news column is almost required these days, although, again, the information should be presented concisely and clearly. Especially useful are LEXIS and Westlaw comparisons, search tips, print charges, and database content news. The announcement should include the library's telephone number as a help line, along with that of the customer service representatives.

Some firm librarians also include news clippings or bibliographical citations to articles about the university, firm, or company. Similarly, the newsletter may contain a column such as "Among Our Authors."

Because the newsletter is both a current awareness and a marketing tool, a sentence or two advertising the library's services should be included in each issue. A simple sentence about the ability to search for data on expert witnesses, especially for opposing sides, is a good example.

A common error of library newsletters is printing information of interest to librarians rather than patrons. The librarian should always remember to ask "Will they care?" before printing anything. Too much "nonsense" will actually be detrimental. With virtually all correspondence that leaves the library, the librarian must take the time to proofread and make it presentable.

Clipping Services

One of the most burdensome and time-consuming tasks in many special libraries is a current awareness service. Many libraries provide a daily or weekly watch service in which they read papers and journals and clip and distribute articles of interest to various people.

This service, for all its headaches, is a marvelous way to earn recognition. When material is sent from the library, it should clearly indicate that it came from the library. Many of the databases now have automatic saved searches that can be run daily, weekly, monthly, or on command. In the law field, the most notable are the LEXIS/NEXIS' ECLIPSE and Westlaw's PDQ. These features can reduce the burden on the staff if a day or two of lag time is not critical to the lawyers.

Library Guide

No matter how small the law library, it is necessary to have a guide for the users. This guide should contain maps detailing the collection layout; procedures and policies; and staff names, titles, and telephone numbers. Because it is probably the first material a new lawyer or student sees about the library, it must present a picture of the library as a professional, well-run facility. Policies should be clearly and completely presented, particularly regarding reserving books, signing out books, interlibrary loan policies, routing policies, acquisitions guides, and information about the card catalog.

The Annual Report

An annual report on the law library is a good opportunity to focus on the accomplishments and successes of the library. Information regarding the size of the collection and staff should be included, as should statistical data regarding the use of the library during the year. Technological and space considerations should be included. A management plan for the following year, setting goals and priorities, helps to ensure that staff, users, and administrators are all aware of the library's role within the organization. A five-year plan should also be included to ensure that the librarian and organization keep an eye to the future.

Pathfinders

Many libraries, recognizing the need to educate users, have been providing brief bibliographies or research aids for many years. These documents can also be an effective marketing tool for the librarians and the library. These documents are visible methods of showing off the credentials and skills of the library staff as well as encouraging the use of the collection.

BUDGETING

Law library costs continue to rise well above the consumer price index and above the costs of most other libraries. As a result, budget preparation and justification has become an increasingly complex procedure, requiring that a greater percentage of the librarians' time be spent in analyzing the library's present and future collection requirements.

Factors Affecting Costs of Law Library Collections

The costs of law libraries increase at a higher rate than those of other general or special libraries. The main reason for this difference lies in the nature of legal research tools. Law libraries must collect legal authority—the reported decisions of our courts, statutes, and administrative materials. Each year, the United States courts are experiencing backlogs due to the increase in cases filed. Our society has become a litigious one, and lawsuits are overburdening the courts. At the same time, our society believes in freedom of information and in access to all the decisions of the courts. Therefore, despite the efforts of some judges and judicial systems to reduce the number of published decisions by not printing the routine or unnoteworthy, this movement has met with great resistance. Critics claim that publishing all decisions ensures a greater level of accountability for judges, since accessible written records open judges' opinions to public scrutiny.[1] As a result, law libraries are forced to purchase the books containing all these reported decisions.

Reports of decisions make up the greatest share of the books in most academic law libraries, so when the new reporters are published at a significantly more rapid rate each year, the effect on library budgets is to add an important additional element of cost. The increasing number of citable cases produces

proportionally more indexing materials and digests, more citations, and more materials from which the editors of encyclopedias and selective reporters must select.[2]

The Minnesota State Law Library has calculated that a basic case
law library of federal and all states cases will grow over 264 linear
feet during the next five years. This number is for case reporters
alone.[4] The proliferation of cases brought to the courts has resulted
in an increase in virtually all types of legal publications. Today's
law librarians, faced with the rapid and continuous rise of costs of
primary authority, are becoming increasingly cautious in selecting
secondary materials, such as treatises, looseleafs, and periodicals.
In addition, they are focusing attention on alternative formats, such
as on-line resources, CD-ROMs, and microfilm and microfiche, as
the only affordable methods of acquiring certain materials.

The Law Library Budget on the Rise

Law library budgets vary greatly due to the wide variety and
scope of their clientele and collections. Among law schools, the
smallest collections had fewer than 100,000 volumes with a median
budget of $293,000 in 1986-87, while the largest schools had li-
brary budgets over $4,000,000. The average increase in all law
school library budgets from 1976 to 1986, regardless of size, however, was 198%.[3] Law firm and corporate law department libraries,
regardless of the size of their collections, have also faced large budget increases from year to year.

The latest price index for legal publications covers 1988-89.[5]
While the costs of legal serials slowed down in 1988 and 1989, the
cost per title has risen 29% in the last five years, from a mean cost
per title of $153.11 in 1984-85 to $197.49 in 1988-89. These escalating prices result in libraries having fewer titles on hand to meet
the needs of the lawyers. To make more material available, librarians are taking a close look at excessive supplementation, dual or
overlapping coverage, and other legal publishing practices and are
alerting publishers to their concern. The FTC Guidelines for the
Law Book Industry,[6] developed in 1975 following complaints from
lawyers and law librarians, are again the focus of those who are
involved with law library budgeting and collection development.

One popular and active arm of the American Association of Law Libraries is the Committee on Relations with Publishers and Dealers, which closely monitors the advertising, promotion, pricing and billing practices of law book vendors.

The Need for a Budget

A budget is an estimated projection of the expenses the library will incur over a given period, usually one year. It is based on prior expenses, anticipated changes, and estimated inflation, and it is useful for planning not only expenses but growth and direction of the library's collection, staffing, service levels, space, and technology. Although often regarded with dread, it is actually a valuable tool for communicating with upper-level management and for ensuring that the future of the library is carefully planned. Goals and objectives, even if not formally stated, are requirements for preparing an accurate and complete budget. If the budget is rejected by the administration of the school, court, bar, or other parent institution, it is usually a signal that the goals and objectives of the library are not in line with those of the organization.

Preparing a Budget

The librarian who must establish a written budget for the first time would be well-advised to consult the law library and accounting literature. Briefly, the first step in preparing a budget is to track expenses over the previous year and to analyze them by category. The expense categories will vary depending upon the organization's requirements, and should be formally established with finance or accounting personnel. Law libraries often track expenses by type of material, with categories such as case reporters, statutes, looseleaf services, treatises, and databases, although some review costs by allocating them to different departments or subject areas (such as litigation, corporate, and tax).

To determine future costs, a careful review of prior expenses should be performed. Law librarians who have several years of data to review are especially fortunate, although simply estimating expenses by multiplying present costs against inflation is a method sure to fail. As previously discussed, law library expenses are always higher than the rate of inflation. Second, such a process does not consider the purchase of new materials. The librarian must review collection weaknesses and identify any areas where new titles or series will need to be added. Similarly, there should be some weeding each year to cancel expensive, little-used sets. Consideration of new technologies may also result in an increase (and rarely a decrease) in library costs.

Types of Budgets

Various types of budgets exist, although many law libraries incorporate several methods into one. The line item budget provides a breakdown of expenses by type of material or department. The program budget examines anticipated expenses associated with the implementation of a special project or program during the year. For example, a retrospective conversion project to automate a card catalog would include personnel, equipment, and related costs.

Presenting the Budget

A written document is usually required when presenting the budget. As with all publications emanating from the law library, it must be neat, accurate, and complete. A combination of textual explanation and statistical data should supplement the budget data. Historical data, incorporating dollars and percentages, should provide a clear, concise picture of the library. Comparisons of the expenses of similar law libraries may be used to support the proposed budget, as may price indices and other published data. Whether the budget is presented orally or not, the law librarian should be prepared to support and justify every piece of the budget.

Monitoring the Budget

Analyzing and reviewing expenses on a monthly basis can help to establish expense patterns and can provide a means of ensuring that expenses are in line with projections. If expenses are significantly higher or lower than expected, the librarian should carefully review the detailed expenses of the categories in question. The librarian should determine the cause(s) and take corrective action or contact the administrators to explain cost overruns before they are recognized by financial personnel or administrators. Being aware of the problem before others helps librarians take the time to examine the discrepancy and make recommendations before administrators become concerned and make hasty, uninformed decisions.

REFERENCE NOTES

1. See, for example: Robel, Lauren K. The myth of the disposable opinion: unpublished opinions and government litigants in the United States Courts of Appeals. *Michigan Law Review.* 87(5):940-962; 1989 April.
2. Schultz, Jon S. Effective book lost analysis and reflections on the American Bar Association Standards. *Law Library Journal.* 75:146-147; 1982.
3. Hammond, Jane L. Library costs as a percentage of law school budgets. *Law Library Journal.* 80:439-445; 1988.
4. Golden, Barbara L. 1989 Space requirements and price list. *Legal Reference Services Quarterly.* 9(3/4):271-281; 1989.
5. Scott, Bettie. Price index for legal publications, 1988-89. *Law Library Journal.* 82:193-196; 1990.
6. Federal Trade Commission. *Guidelines for the law book industry.* Washington: The Commission; 1975 August 8. Also contained in 16 C.F.R. Part 256.

BIBLIOGRAPHY

Anspach, Judith; Stone, Dennis J. The impact of technology on space planning. *Trends in Law Library Management and Technology.* 1(3):6-7; 1987 October. The author predicts that books will remain and computer equipment will increase space requirements for reader stations.

Arranging, moving and maintaining the library. *In:* Finley, Elizabeth. *Manual of procedures for private law libraries.* South Hackensack, NJ: Published for the American Association of Law Libraries by F.B. Rothman; 1966, p. 19-27; and Dyer, Susan K. *Manual of procedures for private law libraries, 1984 supplement,* p.8-17. This practical handbook sets out major techniques, points to consider, and pitfalls in planning, designing, or moving a law firm library.

Burwell, Helen. Cost containment: the ongoing struggle. *In: Managing the private law library 1988.* New York: Practising Law Institute; 1988. p. 117-122. The outline suggests ways in which a law firm librarian can reduce costs.

Cottingham, Jennifer. A new look for the library. *In: Office design for law firms.* New York: National Law Journal; 1988. This article discusses major issues facing designers, including compact shelving and planning for new technologies, and presents several examples of recently designed firm libraries.

Drews, Jeanne. Computers: planning for disaster. *Law Library Journal*. 81:103-116; 1989.

The author advises librarians to incorporate computer hardware, software, and databases in a disaster plan.

Fire, water and smoke protection. *In*: Marke, Julius J.; Sloane, Richard. *Legal research and law library management*. New York: Law Journal Seminars Press; 1982, p. 386-397.

The authors discuss a fire at a New York City high-rise building that housed . several law firms. The experiences of those firm libraries are reviewed, and the authors suggest preventive measures.

French, Sharon K. The annual report of the private law library: a checklist of considerations. *In*: *Managing the private law library: delivering information services*. New York: Practising Law Institute; 1989, p. 491-500.

The author explains why an annual report is beneficial and presents a checklist of contents.

Fu, Paul S. Handling water damage in a law library. *Law Library Journal*. 79:667-687; 1987.

The author, law librarian at the Supreme Court of Ohio Law Library, lived through water damage caused by a broken pipe. He discusses the causes for disaster, as well as how to plan for and react during such an emergency.

Genovese, Robert. A disaster preparedness manual, parts 1 and 2. *Trends in Law Library Management and Technology*. 2(8):1-2; 1989 April and 2(7):1-3; 1989 March.

This two-part article discusses the reason for a disaster preparedness manual and the development process at the University of Arizona College of Law Library.

Grossman, George S. Housing books. *Law Library Journal*. 79:521-533; 1987.

The author questions old formulas for determining space needs, arguing that technology has changed the rules.

Grunenwald, Joseph P.; & Traynor, Kenneth. A Marketing plan for the law library. *Law Library Journal*. 79(1):93-101; 1987.

This article discusses the research, strategic decision making, attention to patron needs, and promotional materials required to undertake a successful marketing plan.

Hammond, Jane L. Library costs as a percentage of law school budgets. *Law Library Journal*. 80:439-45; 1988.

The author reviews law school library budgets and determines that the percentage of the school's budget spent on the library is closer to 10%, not the 20% that most people believed was the benchmark.

King, Dwight. Library budgeting for law librarians: a selected bibliography, 1965-1986. *Law Library Journal*. 80:291-305; 1988.

This excellent annotated bibliography includes both law librarianship and general library literature on all aspects of budgeting.

Law libraries' crisis: rising costs for books and journals. *In*: Marke, Julius J.;

Sloane, Richard. *Legal research and law library management*. New York: Law Journal Seminars Press; 1982, p. 327-333.

The authors explore the reasons for the rapid rise of law books and serials costs and the resultant crisis in law libraries.

Marke, Julius J. A problem for law librarians. *New York Law Journal*. p. 4, col. 4, 1981 Nov. 17.

The author describes the hidden costs of law library collections, including postage, revised volumes, and related titles, which wreak havoc on the law library budget.

Marke, Julius J.; Henke, Dan F. *Planning the law library as a legal information center*. London; New York: Glanville; 1985.

This softcover book discusses the recommended guidelines for planning a state-of-the-art law school library.

Morris, John. *The library disaster preparedness handbook*. Chicago: American Library Association; 1986.

This handbook, intended for libraries of all types, includes chapters on problem patrons, theft, mutilation, fire and water, as well as on safety, preservation, and conservation.

Moynihan, Mary K. Budget development for a law library. *In: The private law firm library: an integral tool of the law firm*. New York: Practising Law Institute; 1977, p.223-247.

The author describes the purpose and types of law library budgets and suggests practical ways to budget more effectively.

Reams, Bernard D; Surrency, Edwin C. *Insuring the law library: fire and disaster risk management*. London; New York: Glanville Publishers; 1982.

This book contains much information on the history and overview of disasters in libraries, insurance, and valuation. Although primarily addressing the academic law library, this guide is useful to any library.

Schultz, Jon S. Effective book cost analysis and reflections on the American Bar Association Standards. *Law Library Journal*. 75:141-147; 1982.

The author explains how the growth in legal authority, such as case reports, has developed and its impact on the law library budget.

Scott, Bettie. Price index for legal publications, 1988-89. *Law Library Journal*. 82:193-196; 1990.

This annual review of law and law-related treatises, periodicals, looseleafs, and court reporters has been published since 1974 and is the authoritative price index for legal materials.

Scott, Carolyn. Managing the library after a disaster. *In: Managing the private law library: delivering information services*. New York: Practising Law Institute; 1989, p. 33-52.

The author presents an outline, checklist and bibliography on disaster planning.

Seer, Gitelle. The law firm library budget: a systematic approach. In: *Private law librarians, 1986*. New York: Practising Law Institute; 1986, p. 367-386.

The author presents, in outline form, many useful ideas for developing and using a budget in law firm libraries.

Sidford, Jill. Beyond the brochure: the library's role in marketing the law firm library of the nineties. In: *Managing the private law library: delivering information services*. New York: Practising Law Institute; 1989, p. 399-414.
This article presents practical approaches to marketing and includes a good selective bibliography.

Sloane, Richard. Fire in the Library—lessons for law firms. *New York Law Journal*. p. 4, col. 1, 1986 Jul. 15.
The author discusses several library disasters and recommends fire avoidance steps, keeping an inventory, and valuing the library.

Stone, Dennis J. Marketing as an integral part of law library management. *Law Library Journal*. 79(1):103-113; 1987.
Stone provides a brief definition of marketing and explains why law librarians should recognize and use marketing techniques.

Stone, Dennis J.; Anspach, Judith. New standards for space planning. *Trends in Law Library Management and Technology*. 1(2):1-2; 1987 Sept.
The author discusses space guidelines developed for libraries by the Council of Educational Facility Planners International.

Strain, Laura M. Cost control and economics. In: *Private law library, 1980's and beyond*. New York: Practising Law Institute; 1979, p. 205-217.
This author presents an outline of reasons for budgeting and planning, assembling and implementing budgets in law firm libraries.

Wallace, Marie. Disaster recovery planning. In: *Managing the private law library: delivering information services*. New York: Practising Law Institute; 1989, p. 525-540.
The author advises careful disaster planning in an automated office environment.

Wallace, Marie. Mission statements. In: *Managing the private law library: delivering information services*. New York: Practising Law Institute; 1989, p. 477-490.
The author explains the value and contents of mission statements in the law firm library.

When disaster strikes: how to handle law office emergencies. Prepared by the Task Force on Law Office Disaster Planning, the Lawyers' Club of San Francisco. Chicago: American Bar Association; 1988.
This brief manual explores many types of disasters and their effects on law firm operations. Although libraries are not covered separately, the guide provides a glimpse at other management problems regarding disasters.

Zelenko, Barbara J. Lawbook consumers air complaints: the "trouble" with publishers. *Legal Information Alert*. 7(7):1-3,14; 1988 Jul.-Aug.
The author discusses the major complaints of law librarians about publishers.

Chapter 8

Personnel and Staffing Issues

THE MLS

The size of the organization in which the library exists will often be the primary determinant of the size of the library. Whether the library consists of a single librarian or a staff of 50, many lawyers and administrators will not recognize that the librarian in charge should have the MLS. It is very important for the librarian to educate the institution about the need for the degree or significant years of experience. Particularly in small law firm and county law libraries, the sole librarian may in fact be a paralegal or another individual with no library experience. Although there are exceptions, in most cases the needs of the users and the institution would be better met by hiring a professional librarian. The higher salary required by the librarian would be countered by savings in collection development and analysis, improved access to the collection and the unique information retrieval skills of the librarian.

THE JD

In academic institutions, it is increasingly common to find the dual MLS and JD degrees among professional staff. A 1988 study found that 88% of all academic library directors held both a law and library degree.[1] Once found only among the library directors, this joint degree is now found among many of the professional staff. There can be no question that the combined degrees offer an excellent educational background to aid in all aspects of law librarianship, and this trend will probably continue.

In law firms, too, there are increasing numbers of librarians with the two degrees, although the numbers are still small. One reason for the reluctance to hire lawyer-librarians in law firms is the fear that such individuals would rather practice law than focus on library tasks. Another question lawyers raise is why anyone who could practice law would choose librarianship instead. Gradually, this fear and suspicion is being replaced by trust and respect.

CONTINUING EDUCATION

Once out of graduate school, the law librarian is not required to take additional course work to remain abreast of the field, unless such requirements have been established by the individual's employer, most likely in the academic environment. Fortunately, most law librarians recognize the need to attend seminars and classes and to read professional journals on a regular basis.

Many law librarians (or their institutions) become members of the American Association of Law Libraries, a professional organization founded in 1906. Over 4,100 law librarians have joined the association, thereby receiving the quarterly *Law Library Journal* and newsletter. The AALL sponsors an annual meeting during which hundreds of seminars, lectures and workshops are held. It is always well attended and appreciated by its attendees for its high quality programs, social events, and, especially, for the opportunity to exchange ideas informally with colleagues.

Although in recent years there have been discussions about splitting into two organizations—one for law school librarians and one for private law librarians—most members recognize the value of sharing ideas and exchanging information with professionals whose needs and goals are related but not the same as their own. Most law librarians hope that the result of the discussion will be to ensure that the programs and journal address the needs of all types of law librarians equally. In years past, it was argued that the programs and publications were primarily geared toward the academic law librarian, although over half of the association is now comprised of private law librarians. The issue is quite complex, however, since the association has always had difficulty in recruiting volunteers from the private sector to serve on committees or to sit on panels at the conference. Similarly, few private law librarians have submitted articles to the *Law Library Journal*. Because their institutions (law firms, corporations, bar associations) continue to demand a great deal of service, they give librarians little time or encouragement for professional development. Academic institutions, on the other hand, by their very nature, have been supportive of active participation in professional organizations.

Law librarians are increasingly involved with other library associations, such as the Special Libraries Association and American Society for Information Science. In addition, librarians are exploring memberships in the American Association of Law Schools, the American Bar Association, and the Association of Legal Administrators. The American Bar Association recently approved associate status for law librarians, a move which encourages law librarians to participate in the association's activities. These memberships provide dual benefits for librarians: the librarians learn from the other members and increase their visibility among other types of professionals.

Other ways for librarians to develop new skills are to attend programs for paralegals or lawyers or to take advanced course work at a university in librarianship, business, management, computers, or law. Because law librarianship is continuously expanding its scope of responsibility, few librarians will be able to perform well in the future without updating and expanding their skills and knowledge.

BURNOUT

The disillusionment, frustration, boredom, and other emotions associated with burnout have been found among law librarians, although the statistical results of a formal study were fairly low.[2] Law librarians scored low in emotional exhaustion and depersonalization, although some dissatisfaction with opportunities for growth and advancement were evident. Some librarians complained about high expectations from lawyers and their low status and lack of respect within the organization.

Law librarians consider themselves professionals and set unusually high standards for themselves (regardless of the expectations of their institutions). However, their value within the organization is often neglected or unrecognized, and few outside of the library realize the pressures of time, the complexity of research demands, or the need to set priorities. Stress may be the result, especially among those in user service positions where fluctuations in demand are unpredictable because the librarians are frustrated by the heavy demand and by their unrecognized efforts.

Law library directors should ensure that ample support groups and positive feedback are provided to help lower stress, anger, and frustration, and they must seek such support for themselves as well.

CAREER OPTIONS FOR LAW LIBRARIANS

Once a law librarian has reached a plateau within the law library, boredom or dissatisfaction may result. One of the major concerns of librarians today is frustration over career growth and development. Although salaries have improved dramatically in recent years and the demand for law librarians is increasing, the jobs at the top — law library directors and administrators — are often dead ends. These top jobs are attained at an early age, with no promotions beyond them. A 1988 survey found that the average age at which a librarian becomes an academic law library director was 33.[3] What options are available to individuals in those positions or to those who do not wish to become administrators? Although the number of choices is expanding, law librarians must often be prepared to market themselves aggressively to obtain jobs outside the traditional library. They may also need to take course work outside of the profession to prove their worth to employers. Among the most commonly selected options are law library consultant, author or editor of legal or library materials, service bureau employee or manager, database manager, or sales representative for a legal database or publisher.

Many law librarians, however, enjoy their positions and the institutions in which they work. Rather than leaving a good position, some librarians are working to enhance their current roles. Some of the options available in law libraries are job enlargement, job enhancement, job rotation, and work redesign, in which greater autonomy is given to the individual.[4] Law firm and corporate librarians, for example, are becoming records managers as well or are developing in-house litigation support databases or on-line precedents programs. To retain valuable staff members, law library administrators are involving all interested librarians in the planning and ongoing responsibilities of such projects. Similarly, although most academic law library directors do teach legal research or other coursework in the law schools, many encourage others in the library to teach and write, also.

Dick Danner, former editor of the *Law Library Journal*, discussed Robert E. Kelley's *The Gold Collar Worker* in a 1986 editorial. Kelley believes that "organizational goals will be accomplished in the new era only if managers provide an environment where employees feel they can accomplish their personal goals within the organizational setting,"[5] particularly when the work force consists of those involved with creating and using information. As Danner points out, managers must ensure that the skills and energies of law librarians are directed toward the organization while also encouraging personal development.

COMPARABLE WORTH

It has been argued that because librarianship has traditionally consisted largely of women, the salaries for the entire profession have remained lower than the value received. Indeed, in 1986 the American Association of Law Libraries passed a resolution calling for the association to support wage comparability with similar occupations.[6]

Even within the profession, there has been inequality among men and women for job opportunity and pay. In the past, this has been explained by the fact that men in law librarianship were more likely to hold both the MLS and JD and to have spent more years working professionally.[7]

In a 1988 survey of academic law library directors, 61% were male and 39% female. However, when examining academic rank, 65% of male directors were full professors compared with only 29% of females. Of the thirteen directors with no faculty rank, twelve were female. According to this survey, "male directors continue to dominate the profession in nearly every positive category; there are more male directors with more years of experience, higher rank, and more publication credits."[8] In private law libraries, 86.3% of the library directors were women in 1988. However, the average salary of male library directors was nearly $3,000 higher than that of female library directors.[9]

ETHICS AND PROFESSIONAL RESPONSIBILITY

The entire library profession has voiced growing concern about information malpractice and the professional responsibilities of librarians. Law librarians, too, are concerned with the quality of print and on-line data. "Dirty" data, or inaccurate or incomplete information retrieved from an on-line source, is not the only concern facing law librarians, however. For many years, law librarians have faced dilemmas in what they should and should not be asked to do. While their goal has always been to provide a high level of service to patrons, they must walk a fine line between reference service and the unauthorized practice of law. Although they may provide references and citations, prepare bibliographies, and suggest sources, they may not interpret cases or statutes or render opinions or legal advice. On paper, the distinction seems clear, but in practice, law librarians are continuously faced with decisions regarding what is and is not appropriate legal reference service.

Although the American Association of Law Libraries has considered a professional code of ethics and related standards, these documents have never been approved. There has been disagreement over content as well as the assumption of need generally. Furthermore, the ethical standards must relate directly to the needs and values of the parent organization. The goals and objectives of academic, private, and public law libraries, based on patron needs, differ, resulting in variant ethical needs. Because most professions do have a code of ethics, it would be wise for law librarians to be familiar with the American Library Association's Statement on Professional Ethics and the American Bar Association's Canons and to give serious consideration again to their professional responsibility.

Whether a code of ethics is formally adopted by the profession or not, individual law librarians should have a clear understanding of the ethical standards expected of them regarding the levels and limits on reference service, developing and maintaining the collection, making the collection accessible to users, and restricting access to confidential information.

STAFFING

One of the many responsibilities of law library directors and managers is to ensure that the staffing levels meet the needs of the organization, both in numbers and skills. A law library manager must have in place a comprehensive staffing plan. It should begin with the library's official goals and objectives to determine need and include policies and procedures regarding recruiting, hiring, training, evaluating, disciplining, and rewarding employees. Even if the plan itself is not written, the documentation supporting and supplementing the plan should be. Among the documents that should be available are:

1. The library organizational chart, showing lines of reporting and areas of responsibility;
2. Job descriptions, updated annually to reflect accurately the responsibilities and requirements for each position in the library;
3. The library procedures manual, also updated annually, to describe in sufficient detail how each task in the library is performed; and
4. The staff evaluation form(s) so all members of the library are aware of what characteristics will be measured to evaluate their performance.

Perhaps the first step in managing staff is knowing how to obtain approval for hiring someone to work in the library. Because the steps will vary from one institution to another, librarians must find out what documentation and political processes are required to increase staff size. Once the justification has been accepted, the next step is recruitment. Ensuring that ads, agencies, and personnel departments accurately present the job is crucial to a successful search.

Screening applicants is usually first performed by reviewing resumes and is followed by interviews. Open-ended questions that gauge the applicant's prior experience, strengths, weaknesses, goals, and personal characteristics are most valuable. Many librarians, however, neglect to ask questions that measure applicants' reference or technical skills. A few specific questions are recommended to weed out those who can market themselves better than they perform the job. For some positions, it is also possible to give a standardized test, although the librarian must be certain that these tests are not discriminatory in any way. To be certain that the interviewer asks only questions allowed by law, it is important to read and review a book on interviewing techniques.

Once an applicant is hired, an orientation and training program should be followed to ensure that the new employee fully understands the goals, objectives, rules, policies and procedures, and grievance procedures. New employees should be given job descriptions, the organizational chart, and all written documents that describe the library and its policies and procedures. These documents should then be supplemented with formal and informal discussions and meetings. Simply leaving the new employee alone with the procedures manual is a sure way to guarantee the employee's dissatisfaction, alienation, and failure. Feedback and two-way communication should be a regular part of orientation and future supervision.

Performance appraisals should also be part of staff supervision. Despite regular ongoing feedback, problems may remain, or employees may not feel they are recognized or valued. Written and oral evaluations in a formal setting indicate to employees that managers recognize strengths and weaknesses and that they will work with employees to improve performance and development.

Occasionally, despite all the manager's efforts, an employee's performance is unacceptable. Disciplinary procedures in accordance with those of the parent institution are essential to a guilt-free, legally sound termination of an employee. Although the manager should feel unhappy about firing an individual, there should be no doubt that ample warnings and counseling were attempted. In today's litigious society, disciplinary documentation should precede an employee's termination.

One aspect of library personnel management often overlooked in smaller libraries is grievance procedures. It is important to develop authorized ways for staff to register complaints against the library manager, other staff, or what the employee perceives to be inequitable treatment or policies.

None of the principles discussed here is unique to law librarianship. Unfortunately, law librarians in managerial and administrative positions do not always have much education or experience in managing people. Although the library schools are focusing more attention on such issues, the responsibility for learning lies with the librarians themselves. Library managers, or those aspiring to the position, should read management literature on a regular basis and should apply the principles and practices in their libraries.

REFERENCE NOTES

1. Slinger, Michael J. The career paths and education of current academic law library directors. *Law Library Journal.* 80(2):217-239; 1988.
2. Nelson, Veneese C. Burnout: a reality for law librarians. *Law Library Journal.* 79(2):267-275; 1987.
3. Slinger, Michael J. The career paths and education of current academic law library directors. *Law Library Journal.* 80(2):217-239; 1988.
4. Schanck, Peter C. Designing enriched jobs in law libraries. *Law Library Journal.* 78(3):375-404; 1986.
5. Danner, Dick. From the editor: gold-collar librarians. *Law Library Journal.* 78(2):213-217; 1986.
6. Johnson, Nancy P. Comparable worth in libraries: a legal analysis. *Law Library Journal.* 79(3):367-386; 1987.
7. Carrick, Kathleen. Silk v. corduroy: the status of men and women in librarianship. *Law Library Journal.* 78(3):425-441; 1986.
8. Slinger, Michael J. The career paths and education of current academic law library directors. *Law Library Journal.* 80(2):217-239; 1988.
9. *Private law libraries: a survey of compensation, operations and collections.* 1988 ed. Conducted by Altman & Weil for the American Association of Law Libraries, Private Law Libraries Special Interest Section. Ardmore, PA: Altman & Weil; 1988.

BIBLIOGRAPHY

Carrick, Kathleen. Silk v. corduroy: the status of men and women in law librarianship. *Law Library Journal.* 78(3):425-441; 1986.
The author compares the membership of the American Association of Law Libraries in 1971 and 1982 to determine changes in the sex, age, experience, and educational levels of its membership. Women were still in lower job types, with lower salaries, showing little improvement over the same observation made in 1904.
Danner, Dick. From the editor: gold-collar librarians. *Law Library Journal.* 78(2):213-217; 1986.
Danner discusses Robert E. Kelley's book, *The Gold-Collar Worker,* as it relates to law librarianship. Kelley sees today's employee as expecting to meet his/her own personal goals in addition to those of the organization. Since this

phenomena is most pronounced in those who create or use information, law
library managers must develop innovative ways to ensure that both the individual's and the organization's needs are met.

Ethical problems of law librarianship. *Law Library Journal*. 67(4):528-540; 1974.
   This panel discussion followed a draft of a code of professional ethics for law
   librarians that was never passed. Many interesting viewpoints are presented
   as to what should or should not be included in such a code as well as reasons
   for and against a code.

Heroy, Donna Tuke. New functions and expanding roles for private law librarians. *Legal Information Alert* 8(4):1-3; 1989 April.
   The author discusses the trend toward new titles and new responsibilities for the
   private law librarians.

Johnson, Nancy P. Comparable worth in libraries: a legal analysis. *Law Library
   Journal*. 79(3):367-386; 1987.
   Johnson defines comparable worth and identifies reasons why librarianship as a
   profession suffered a wage gap. She also examines the leading cases of comparable work.

Lee, Frank. Expanding your base: the law librarian as records manager. *Law
   Library Journal*. 80(1)123-129; 1988.
   The author describes the role of records manager in the law firm and provides
   reasons why the librarian is a logical choice for the job.

Leone, Gerome. Malpractice liability of a law librarian? *Law Library Journal*.
   73(1):44-65; 1980.
   The author examines the remote possibility of a law librarian being sued for
   malpractice. He questions what duty is created by the librarian—patron rela-
   tionship and discusses the formal and informal standards of law librarianship.

Mills, Robin K. Reference service vs. legal advice: is it possible to draw the line?
   Law Library Journal. 72(2):179-193; 1979.
   The author recognizes that law librarians, particularly in public law libraries, do
   occasionally cross the line in providing library assistance to the unauthorized
   practice of law. Several partial solutions are suggested, but the author ulti-
   mately questions the role public law librarians should play.

Schanck, Peter C. Designing enriched jobs in law libraries. *Law Library Journal*.
   78(3):375-404; 1986.
   Schanck maintains that job satisfaction and productivity can be enhanced by
   redesigning jobs to allow greater autonomy.

Sinder, Janet. Law library management: an annotated bibliography. *Law Library
   Journal* 81:567-578; 1989.
   The author has divided articles into several management categories: general,
   budgeting, communications, personnel, and technology.

Wallace, Marie. Ethics: is it time for a code? *In*: *Managing the private law library
   1988*. New York: Practising Law Institute; 1988, p. 329-340.
   Wallace reviews the history of debates regarding standards and a professional
   code of ethics and concludes that the profession needs to reopen the discussions.

Chapter 9

Special Issues
for Law Firm Libraries

CLIENT BILLING

Historically, law firm library costs were considered unrecoverable overhead, but more and more firms are realizing that although the library will not likely become a profit center, there are certainly some expenses that can be billed to clients. For years, lawyers and many other professionals have billed clients for their time by establishing hourly fees. In the last decade or so, most large law firms and some smaller ones have expanded their billing practices to include some support personnel. The change came with much controversy, however, as many lawyers (and clients) believed that the support departments should be considered an overhead expense that was already indirectly charged to the client through the lawyer's high fees. Today, many law firm administrators argue that it is less expensive and more cost efficient for the client to pay the support personnel's hourly charge than the lawyer's, but the debate continues. With the advent of librarians "diarying" their time came several difficult questions: (1) what is a fair charge? and (2) what assignments are billable?

The firm's billing committee or library committee determines the fair rates for all support personnel. Hourly fees for librarians in New York City ranged from as low as $25 to as much as $85 in 1988, with most other cities somewhat lower. This compares with rates for lawyers that range from $77 to $400 in New York, with similar or slightly lower rates elsewhere in the country.[1] Librarian rates are generally compared to, and sometimes equivalent to, paralegal rates within the firm.

A far more difficult question is the decision to charge for a particular library service, and this decision is frequently at the discretion of the librarian. Even if policies are written, their interpretation is difficult. Practices vary from firm to firm. Some charge only for time spent on research, while others charge for ready reference and retrieval as well. Most charge for the time spent locating a book through interlibrary loan and for the librarian's time spent on databases. Some firms charge for librarians (or pages) to retrieve and deliver books to lawyers.

Although the librarian, trained in a service-oriented profession, may initially react with reservations or guilt about such detailed billing practices, the alternative would cost a client more. For a librarian (or page) to pull and deliver a volume at $50 per hour is less expensive for the client than a lawyer coming in to get it himself or herself at $150 per hour. The librarian is actually saving the client money because the lawyer would certainly charge his time to the client. But what about when the volume requested is off the shelf? Should the client then pay for the librarian to track it down from another lawyer or through interlibrary loan? In such cases, most librarians charge clients only for the estimated time the request would have required under normal circumstances, rather than for the actual time spent.

Most librarians, although initially reluctant to begin the tedious record keeping required to diary time, learn to appreciate the practice. At first, lawyers are resistant to providing client names and numbers, but most adjust as the librarians make it part of every reference interview. A few lawyers, for a variety of reasons, never do provide numbers. Librarians quickly realize, however, that there are several excellent reasons for adopting good billing practices:

1. Lawyers and administrators hold the library staff in higher esteem as they begin to accept the librarian as part of the professional team with valuable services to offer the client.
2. Sometimes knowing the client and matter can help the librarian better understand the research assignment.
3. Librarians feel more satisfaction when they look at the diary and realize the number and variety of assignments they have

handled in a day. Their sense of self-worth is frequently higher after a billing time policy is instituted.

4. The library now has a quantifiable tool for the firm's management group to review to help determine the library's performance and value.

5. The time diaried to clients helps (directly or indirectly, depending upon the firm's budgeting practice) to offset the librarians' salaries. In a few firms, the librarians' billing practices result in net income for the firm.

CONFIDENTIALITY AND SECURITY ISSUES

Law firm and corporate legal department librarians are part of a team whose goal is to meet the legal needs of the firm or company. Oftentimes, those needs are urgent and sensitive. The librarian's role is to gather facts in a way that does not alert others or draw attention to the client or issue. For example, locating environmental laws and regulations relating to transporting hazardous waste may need to be done anonymously or without outside assistance. Otherwise, it is possible that the media or opposing counsel could learn of your information request and base an investigation on such a tip. Use of document delivery companies or service bureaus is one way to ensure anonymity.

One dilemma law librarians sometimes face is whether, in attempting to locate information, they should lie about their identities. This technique may be used to protect the confidentiality of the client or company from the public or from opposing counsel. It is also used to obtain information that would not usually be given without clearance from the information giver's supervisor. Each librarian must decide upon the best course of action based on the situation.

Each day, law librarians are privy to a great deal of confidential information. Such information may be simple gossip which will leak soon enough (such as divorce proceedings for public figures), or it may never be disclosed. Law librarians must always assume that their research is extraordinarily sensitive information, regardless of how bland it may seem. This is the only way to ensure that the client's or company's privacy is protected. Although basic information needs regularly require contacting other information professionals, such outside sources must be approved in advance by the person requesting the information.

Even within the organization, law librarians must quickly learn that client matters or legal department issues are not to be discussed with others. In large law firms, especially, what one group of lawyers is working on may be top secret. In a hostile takeover bid, for example, or in any kind of merger or acquisition, there is no such think as an innocent leak. Stockholders or investors stand to lose or gain millions of dollars on the stock market if someone divulges information about proposed or pending corporate deals.

More and more law librarians are taking precautions to keep their work quiet. Individual offices, once unheard of in law firms especially, are increasingly more common. There, reference interviews, computer and print research, and telephone calls can be handled without alerting others. Reference logs and pending research can be kept under lock.

Although always of concern to lawyers, computer database security is often questioned by librarians as well. Library users, even in libraries off limits to outside visitors, are advised regularly to take papers with them.

Finally, paper shredders are making their way into libraries.

REPRESENTING THE UNPOPULAR CLIENT

Most law librarians, like librarians generally, did not enter the field to get rich. Most were attracted by the more noble goal of providing improved access to information or the challenge of answering the impossible question. Somewhere along the way, however, law librarians in corporate legal departments and law firm librarians may be uncomfortable with their assignments. What does the librarian do when asked to help locate a loophole for the swindler, convicted rapist, child molester, or terrorist? How does a law firm librarian reconcile the discrepancy between the legal representation provided to a multibillion dollar corporation versus the indigent petty thief? Like lawyers themselves, law librarians must accept a professional code of responsibility to use all their abilities and resources to their fullest, regardless of their personal beliefs about the client. The decision to accept or reject a client is not the librarian's. If the librarian works in an organization that he or she feels does not balance the profitable representation of wealthy clients with pro bono (for the good of the people) matters, the obvious alternative is to seek employment elsewhere. Another option may be to volunteer time and services to a legal aid clinic or organization that represents a group or cause that the librarian supports. Once the librarian has agreed to work in a company or firm, he or she must not compromise or cut corners on the quality of the work regardless of perceived injustice.

MANAGING BRANCHES

Law firms and corporations often have their headquarters in one location and smaller satellites or branches in other buildings, cities, states, or countries. Branching out is now one of the major methods of expansion seen among today's law firms. Less than a decade ago, if a law firm had a branch office at all, it was a small Washington, D.C. outpost. Today, nearly all of the 200 largest law firms in the United States have at least one branch. Many have both foreign and domestic offices. The legal field has seen tremendous growth in international practice which brought about a need for local experts. On the domestic scene, many law firms have gone national by opening one or more branches on the opposite coast and by staffing midwestern and southern cities as well. These branch offices are seen as an important way to generate new business and retain clients located in these branch locations, but they also cause many managerial problems.

For the headquarters librarian, the problems are numerous. If the branch office is small, the librarian may be expected to provide long distance service. Research and reference work must be handled via phone, fax, and mail service, often resulting in stressful time constraints and communications problems. Trying to make the express mail pick-up and working with different time zones are just two of the added stress factors when working with branch lawyers. Arranging an interlibrary loan from another city is another, and it requires that the headquarters librarian know at least two cities' library resources.

If the branch office is to have a library, the headquarters librarian may be expected to design the space. This is very difficult without knowing the work habits, personalities, and needs of the local lawyers but is preferable to being assigned inadequate space. Similarly, the librarian may be responsible for collection development, paying of invoices, and even check-in and routing operations.

In larger branch offices, the library is often large enough to require a branch librarian and/or library staff. In the best situations, this results in cooperative acquisitions, shared resources, frequent brainstorming between librarians, routine sharing of ideas, and the development of policies, procedures, goals, and objectives. Although the headquarters librarian is often still expected to develop and implement a branch library budget and supervise branch library staff, the reporting line may instead be to a branch office administrator. In any case, frequent two-way communication is essential to a successful, coordinated library.

MERGERS

Law firms and corporations have also experienced significant change in structure in recent years due to "mergermania." Law firms and major corporations struggling for financial strength and survival have adopted a bigger is better philosophy. These organizations have found many advantages to acquiring a ready-made practice or company. For many special librarians, these friendly and hostile takeovers have caused much concern. For the librarian in either a target or acquirer's library, the resulting merger will inevitably bring change. Hopefully, the librarian's job security is not at stake, although the merging of the firms often means that the library staff and collections are combined, with elimination of duplicates. Staff may be laid off or job descriptions rewritten. Most likely one head librarian will be placed in charge and new reporting lines will be established. Inevitably, the new, combined firm or company philosophy will differ from one or both of the old organizations' philosophies, resulting in new politics and policies for the library as well. Among the organizational changes for the librarian are: status of the library—where does it fit in the organization?; litigation support—is this a library responsibility?; precedents collections and/or brief banks — is this a library responsibility? Internally, the librarians will need to review all procedures and politics, from acquisitions to weeding. The librarian placed in charge of the new firm's library or libraries must adapt to the many changes and will need to be diplomatic to both old and new staff and lawyers.

DISSOLVING THE LIBRARY

Law firms and corporations occasionally dissolve, most often due to a merger or breakup of a partnership.[2] In either case, the librarian's role of closing down the library is very challenging. The first step for the librarian is to inventory the collection, beginning with a complete recall of books in use. Next, the librarian may wish to contact a broker or dealer to assist in valuing and disposing of the collection. Books may be sold to the firm or corporation's lawyers, to other firms, or to a dealer. In any case, publishers should be notified to stop sending supplements or to transfer accounts to the new owners. Among the most difficult tasks are paying all outstanding invoices and making the physical arrangements to pack up and turn over the collection. One might argue that there is nothing as challenging as starting a library, but the entire process of dissolving a law library is even more intellectually, physically, and emotionally trying.

SUMMER ASSOCIATES

Law firm libraries, unlike academic law libraries, are often busiest in the summer, especially in May, June, and July. This is the season in which firms hire law school students who have completed their second year of law school. These summer law clerks or summer associates are hired to give the firm and the students a chance to decide whether or not they will make a suitable match the following year when the students seek permanent positions. These law clerks are given a balance of real legal work and social activities aimed at wooing them. Among the least favorite activities of most summer clerks is library research. They want to spend time in the courtroom, meet with clients and partners, and be involved in more exciting, visible work. Their disappointment with research assignments, combined with very limited practical research experience, makes the librarian's role very stressful and frustrating. The student's disappointment with the assignment does not alter his or her goal of impressing the firm with outstanding work, so the student often places very high expectations of service and assistance on the librarian.

Law librarian burnout in firms (and to a lesser extent corporate legal departments which hire summer law clerks in fewer numbers) is probably highest in June. The librarian's job, already a full-time workload, must expand to fill the needs of the added user population during the season in which the American Association of Law Libraries' annual meeting is held and most people make vacation plans. With law school students working in major city firms earning well over $1,000 per week, it is the time when law librarians most need each other's support and the firm's recognition of their performance. Unfortunately, most support comes from other law librarians, since firm administrators rarely recognize the summer associate program's impact on the library or other service departments.

TEACHING LEGAL RESEARCH

Although many people would argue that teaching legal research belongs in the law schools, the fact is that even under ideal circumstances, lawyers cannot ever stop learning legal research tools and techniques. Lawyers will be required to gain knowledge and skill throughout their careers, and part of the responsibility for teaching will fall increasingly upon the law firm or corporate law librarian.

As new print and online tools and methods are developed, the librarian must disseminate the information and assist lawyers in using these products and procedures. Cost consciousness and selectivity will also be aspects of legal research that librarians must teach. All legal materials are expensive, but especially costly are online databases. Most would argue that academic online research training is woefully inadequate in discussing the costs and cost-cutting techniques of computer research. Additionally, the proliferation of legal research materials and increasing reliance upon non-legal databases and print resources already requires that the lawyer be selective and know what to use and when to stop acquiring materials. Law librarians must be able to teach lawyers how to evaluate and select the valuable resources and how to eliminate the overload. Finally, law librarians whose users are practicing lawyers must educate or re-educate lawyers in the use of traditional print materials. In recent years, these traditional resources have been less stressed in law schools as computer-assisted legal research moved to the forefront. A common concern among librarians and experienced lawyers is that new lawyers do not go beyond the computer terminal to research a topic, presumably under the mistaken belief that if it exists, it is online. Combating the lack of research expertise among lawyers is a job for all librarians, not simply those in the academic environment.

REFERENCE NOTES

1. Special survey: billing. *National Law Journal*. Special Supp. S1-S12; 1988 Nov. 7; and Billing rates at 47 U.S. law firms. *Of Counsel*. 7(5):8-10; 1988 Mar.
2. Chicco, Meg. Closing down: the book sale. *In*: *Private law libraries, 1986*. New York: Practising Law Institute; 1986, p. 219-226.

BIBLIOGRAPHY

Ahrens, Barbara. Branch libraries. *In*: *Managing the private law library, 1988*. New York: Practising Law Institute; 1988, p.21-26.
   The author briefly describes the development of a branch library and the problems that arise in managing it.
Axelroth, Joan L. Library instruction in the private law firm environment. *Legal Reference Services Quarterly*. 5(2/3):117-176; 1985 Summer/Fall.
   The author discusses the need for in-house library instruction and presents a model program.
Billing clients for library service. *In*: Marke, Julius J.; Sloane, Richard. *Legal research and law library management*. New York: Law Journal Seminars-Press; 1982, p. 365-368.
   The authors present advantages and disadvantages of billing librarians' time to clients.
Chicco, Meg. Closing down: the book sale. *In*: *Private law librarians 1986*. New York: Practising Law Institute; 1986, p. 219-226.
   This brief article was written by a librarian who dissolved a law firm's library.
Davidson, Donald S. Branch libraries: a branch librarian's perspective. *In*: *Private law librarians 1986*. New York: Practising Law Institute; 1986, p. 243-269.
   The author presents an outline of the ideal responsibilities of a branch librarian

and has compiled a selected annotated bibliography of material on law firm branch offices.

Lastres, Steven A. Surviving the merger: living with branch libraries. *In: Managing the private law library: delivering information services*. New York: Practising Law Institute; 1989, p.27-32.

This chapter is a brief outline of steps required to prepare for a merger. It also discusses different levels of service and maintaining peer relationships and communications with branch libraries.

The law firm library of the future: technology takes research beyond the bookshelves. Pull-out management report. *American Lawyer*. 1988 Dec. 18 pages.

This article discusses, among other things, billing practices and policies among large law firm libraries.

Lewis, Nancy J. Legal research training programs for attorneys. *In: Managing the private law library: delivering information services*. New York: Practising Law Institute; 1989, p. 307-316.

The author describes a survey of librarians' perceptions of legal research needs and presents a recommended program for in-house training.

Palmer, Catherine C. Branches and twigs, or how to survive firm expansion. *In: Private law librarians 1986*. New York: Practising Law Institute; 1986, p. 227-241.

The author presents, in outline form, various scenarios of firm expansion and the librarian's role in establishing adequate library operations.

Passing on costs II: law firms tread lightly with library services. *Of Counsel*. 7(12):1, 9-10; 1988 June.

This article surveys billing practices of law firm libraries and describes some of the philosophies associated with them.

Piper, Larry W. Dealing with a merger. *In: Managing the private law library 1988*. New York: Practising Law Institute; 1988, p.67-72.

The author of this outline presents questions to ask and problems to address before and during a merger.

Rock, Harold L. Branch office libraries or a tale of five cities. *In: Private law library 1980's and beyond*. New York: Practising Law Institute; 1979, p. 175-195.

This article presents one firm librarian's experiences in managing multiple branch libraries.

Rosenfeld, Leslie A. Services to foreign branch offices. *In: Managing the private law library: delivering information services*. New York: Practising Law Institute; 1989, p. 285-290.

The author presents, in outline form, the steps in selecting and acquiring materials and in handling information requests for foreign branch office staff.

Sheeler, Harva L. After the merger: the law library. *In: Managing the private law library 1988*. New York: Practising Law Institute; 1988, p. 73-93.

The author presents a thorough review of library operations affected by a law firm merger.

Whitaker, Carl. Branch libraries. *In*: Dyer, Susan K., ed. *Manual of procedures for private law libraries, 1984 supplement*. Littleton, CO: Published for the American Association of Law Libraries by F. B. Rothman; 1984, p. 66-68.

The author of this chapter discusses collection development, space planning, staffing and maintenance, and reporting structure as the primary issues of branch library management.

Chapter 10

Special Issues
for Academic Law Libraries

ACCREDITATION OF LAW SCHOOL LIBRARIES

For many years, the American Bar Association and the Association of American Law Schools have promulgated standards for law schools to ensure that the quality of legal education meets minimum requirements. Institutions that do not meet these standards are not accredited by the associations, making their programs undesirable in most parts of the country where graduation from an accredited school is one of the requirements for practicing law. Among the standards of the ABA and AALS are standards relating to the law library. These standards relate to the physical plant, print and non-print collections, and staff and institutional support of the library.

Although the standards are successful in assuring that the institutions provide the resources required to produce competent graduates, many argue that the library standards overemphasize size of the collection over quality. One of the reporting requirements of law school libraries, for example, is volume count, which favors the older and larger law schools such as Harvard and Yale. Newer law school libraries with high quality collections simply cannot compare favorably, despite their excellent services.

Another criticism of the ABA/AALS standards is that volume count is self-reported and may be intentionally or accidentally misstated. Because of the emphasis on quantity, 47% of all academic law library directors reportedly think that some law libraries intentionally misstated volume count.[1] Many more law library directors think that libraries incorrectly reported their volume count because of the confusing and complicated calculations required to compute the volume count.

Nearly all law library directors would like to see a shift away from ABA/AALS standards that measure quantity toward measurements of quality. Factors such as database access, non-print collections, interlibrary loan policies, and hours of library service need to be expanded.

SHARING RESOURCES

Academic law libraries can no longer acquire everything they need. The information explosion has simply made it impossible to afford or house all that is available. Especially in recent years when the interest in foreign and international law has increased, acquisitions decisions have become more difficult. As a result, law school libraries have been examining ways to provide access to materials without purchasing them. One method has been to use databases, but even more common has been the expansion of interlibrary loan and cooperative acquisitions. Major research libraries, as well as smaller specialized libraries, are working with each other to develop policies and plans in which each library purchases unique titles and allows other institutions access to them. With the availability of shared bibliographic utilities, such as RLIN and OCLC, this process is increasingly sophisticated and will continue to be a necessary part of the acquisitions program in the future. Another recent trend is for academic reference librarians to offer fee-based services to law firms, corporations, and individuals to generate funds for acquisitions and staff.

FACULTY STATUS AND TENURE

Although attaining faculty status for head law librarians probably required much effort, it is likely that it was less difficult for them than for university librarians generally. For many years, law library directors have been considered members of the law school and law faculty and have held the law degree. Unlike university librarians, law librarians agreed unanimously to pursue faculty status, and many held teaching responsibilities for many years. Whatever the cause, the result is that even as early as 1973, 86% of academic law library directors held some form of faculty status.[2] An updated survey in 1984 indicated that the number had increased to nearly 94%.[3]

Eighty-two percent of directors are also eligible for tenure. For law librarians other than the head, however, the picture is less clear and the future uncertain. The 1984 survey indicated that only one-third of this group held faculty status or rank, and one-third had or was working toward tenure.

The reasons for the differing treatment of head librarians and their staff is complex and related to each institution's policies. One reason may be the degree requirements, since most heads hold both the MLS and the JD. While growing numbers of academic law librarians who are not directors also hold the dual degrees, the JD is often not required. Secondly, the support librarian may not hold teaching responsibilities. A third problem among many institutions, however, is the question of autonomy. A primary goal of most law school libraries is to be autonomous from the university system. Yet many law school librarians are only eligible for faculty status or tenure through the university plan. Following such a system would often require the law librarians to come under review for faculty status and tenure by the university librarians and deans. It might also place them under the university's tighter salary guidelines or require that law librarians join committees and meet with librarians within the university structure. These requirements often negate the benefits of attaining faculty status and tenure. Unless faculty status can be attained through the law school directly, the percentage of law librarians holding such rank will probably not increase.

TEACHING LEGAL RESEARCH

In many law schools, the task of teaching legal research to law school students has for many years been left to the academic law librarians. They are the logical choice, since their area of expertise is in knowing the content, arrangement, and use of legal research tools. The responsibility for teaching legal research in the law schools is a difficult one, however, and there is increasing concern among practicing lawyers and librarians today that legal research education is failing. The problems are many and complex. Among the complaints are that graduates are unable to use many of the basic tools, that they are not creative in their approach to research, or that they rely too heavily (or exclusively) on computer databases, often without having enough training on search strategies.

The reasons that legal research courses are insufficient are not clear-cut, although there are many published articles that examine the problem. In some cases, the failure is due to the lack of emphasis on and institutional support of the course. Legal research is usually taught in the first year only and is not weighted as heavily as contracts and other substantive law courses. Often, the course is only one semester and is squeezed in among full-year courses. By the time students are expected to use their sources in their second and third years of law school, they have forgotten much of what they have learned.

Another explanation for the problem is the difficulty in covering such a wealth of research tools. Educators say there are simply too many tools to study in detail, so students are only exposed to the rudimentary aspects of sources. Students do not learn about a title in depth nor do they learn alternative sources.

Yet another criticism of legal research courses is the way they are taught. Critics say that tools are taught one by one, rather than in the context of a research problem, so students do not learn creative solutions or, in some cases, current applications of research techniques to the problem.

In response to the criticism, there is renewed interest in teaching legal research in the law schools and beyond. Educators from law schools, law librarians, and practicing lawyers are all interested in improving the legal research skills of new lawyers. As evidence of the focus, the newsletter *Integrated Legal Research*[4] now exists to discuss instruction techniques and theories. A growing number of law schools now offer advanced legal research courses in the second year of the curriculum.

THE STUDENT EMPLOYEE

Law school libraries have been for many years a place for students to work part-time to help finance their educations. In fact, such positions have been sought, as they are preferred to cafeteria or office jobs which look less important and scholarly on the resume. The student employee in the law library is a mixed blessing. On the one hand, students are often bright and able workers who handle mundane tasks (such as filing catalog cards or working at the circulation desk) with ease and without complaint. They can sometimes do more complex tasks as well. Because they are part-time they do not earn benefits or vacation time and are relatively inexpensive labor.

On the negative side, however, students can require an inordinate amount of supervision. Some students think they can do their school work or socialize rather than perform work assignments. Many students only work half-heartedly, reserving their energy for course work, and a large percentage of students inevitably quit at exam time. For the full-time staff, training new people each semester and monitoring their performance can be frustrating. Despite the problems, the student work program is here to stay, and law school libraries should focus attention on improving the quality of the program.

CONSERVATION AND PRESERVATION

Academic law libraries have always maintained some of the finest historical law collections in the country. While law firm and other special law libraries are focused on the practical needs of lawyers, law school libraries emphasize scholarship, comparative law, legal theory, and history. It is not surprising that these institutions are the most concerned with the conservation and preservation of their resources.

A growing number titles in academic library collections are crumbling. Law libraries are faced with the complex task of salvaging the content of these titles in some form or another. One serious source of concern is the use of acidic paper by the Government Printing Office and most private publishers since 1860 and still in use today. After 50 years or less, the paper used to print such important documents as cases, legislative histories, and research papers becomes so brittle that the volumes are unusable. Librarians in all fields must become vocal in their demand that publishers, most especially the GPO, convert to using alkaline paper. According to one author,[5] doing so is not more expensive and is less environmentally hazardous, yet paper manufacturers are only slowly adopting new paper processes because of the one-time conversion costs.

Even if all publishers converted to alkaline paper today, however, titles published for the last 130 years are likely to crumble under routine use. Academic law libraries must institute serious preservation programs to preserve the nation's rich historical legislative materials. They must allocate funds to educating staff and users about handling, microfilming, or converting documents to computer databases. Funding must be sought through grants, endowments, or gifts, or by writing the costs into the budget. A program should include "maintenance, both for circulating materials as well as rare ones; stabilization, including preventive measures, environment monitoring, housing, and handling; security, including disaster planning and theft prevention; and preservation of deteriorating volumes, such as brittle books."[6] Although preservation programs are not new and are not unique to law libraries, they will be a focus of academic law library administration and management in the future.

REFERENCE NOTES

1. Flores, Arturo. Volume count: a survey of practice and opinion from academic law libraries. *Law Library Journal*. 79:241-254; 1987.

2. Bailey, James F.; Dee, Mathew F. Law school libraries: survey relating to autonomy and faculty status. *Law Library Journal*. 67:3-29; 1974.

3. Trelles, Oscar M.; Bailey, James F. Autonomy, librarian status, and librarian tenure in law school libraries: the state of the art, 1984. *Law Library Journal*. 78:605-681; 1986.

4. *Integrated Legal Research*. Quarterly. Dayton: Mead Data Central, Inc. v. 1(1)−;1988 Summer.

5. Nainis, Linda et al. Why GPO should use alkaline paper. *DttP (Documents to the People)* 16:38-41; 1988 Mar.

6. Buchanan, Sally A. Administering the library conservation program. *Law Library Journal*. 77:569-574; 1984-85 at p. 571.

BIBLIOGRAPHY

Anspach, Judith. Effective teaching of legal research in an on-line environment. *Trends in Law Library Management and Technology*. 2(4): 1-3; 1988 Nov.
  The author summarizes the presentations of an October 1988 conference.
Austin, John; Carmencita, K. Cui. Teaching legal research in American law schools: an annotated bibliography. *Legal Reference Services Quarterly*. 7(1):71-83; 1987 Spring.
  This bibliography is a comprehensive annotated list of articles on the teaching of legal research.

Berring, Robert C.; Heuvel, Kathleen Vanden. Legal research: should students learn it or wing it? *Law Library Journal.* 81:431-449; 1989.

The authors take issue with the Wrens' article (see below).

Buchanan, Sally A. Administering the library conservation program. *Law Library Journal.* 77:569-574; 1984-85.

The author briefly describes the cause for concern in law libraries and the points to consider in establishing a successful conservation program.

Carlson, Rhonda; Calvert, Lois; McConkey, Joan. Innovations in legal bibliography instruction. *Law Library Journal.* 74:615-618; 1981.

The authors describe the legal bibliography class at the University of Colorado Law School.

Grossman, George S. Clinical legal education and the law library—an update. *Law Library Journal.* 67:60-78; 1974; Grossman, George S. Clinical legal education and the law library—an update. *Law Library Journal.* 72:75-79; 1979.

The author defines and describes the clinical legal education movement in the U.S.

Howland, Joan. Student employees in the academic law library. *Trends in Law Library Management and Technology.* 1(4):5-8; 1987 Nov.

This excellent article describes the benefits and drawbacks of student employees and offers practical policies and procedures to guide their supervisors.

Integrated Legal Research. Quarterly. Dayton, OH: Mead Data Central, Inc. v. 1(1)—;1988 Summer.

This quarterly newsletter is published and distributed as a public service by Mead Data Central to present techniques of teaching traditional and automated legal research. Each issue is approximately eight pages and presents views from academic and law firm libraries.

Kauffman, S. Blair. Advanced legal research courses: a new trend in American legal education. *Legal Reference Services Quarterly.* 6(3/4):123-139; 1986 Fall/Winter.

The author surveyed law students and describes the advanced legal research courses in place or under consideration in law schools.

Levin, Betsy. Experience, not education. *National Law Journal.* vol: 13; 1989 Feb.

The author, Executive Director of the Association of American Law Schools, explains that the law schools cannot be expected to take the place of experience.

Mills, Robin K. Legal research instruction after the first year of law school. *Law Library Journal.* 76:603-604; 1983.

The author recommends that law school students add an advanced legal research course to the curriculum.

Nainis, Linda et al. Why GPO should use alkaline paper. *DttP (Documents to the People).* 16:38-41; 1988 Mar.

The authors criticize the GPO for using acidic paper in printing and suggests that if GPO converted to alkaline paper, other publishers would follow suit.

Reddy, Michael B. A look at legal research and writing courses. *Legal Information Alert.* 7(2):1-3; 1989 Feb.

The author reviews theories of teaching legal research and advises law librarians to focus on the increasing criticism of law school graduates' legal research skills.

Richard, Paul. Oral competence testing of legal research techniques. *Law Library Journal*. 77:731-736; 1984-85.

The author describes the oral examination process used at the University of Akron School of Law.

White, Emilie. Student assistants in academic law libraries: from reluctance to reliance. *Journal of Academic Librarianship*. 11(2):93-97; 1985 May.

The author briefly describes the history and philosophy behind using student assistants in law libraries and presents the pros and cons of such programs.

Woxland, Thomas A. Why can't Johnny research? or it all started with Christopher Columbus Langdell. *Law Library Journal*. 81:451-464; 1989.

The author surveys the history, successes, and failures of legal research courses.

Wren, Christopher G.; Wren, Jill Robinson. The teaching of legal research. *Law Library Journal*. 80:7-61; 1988.

The authors describe reasons for the failure of traditional legal research courses and present their recommendations regarding how to structure a course.

Chapter 11

Special Issues
for Government-Sponsored
Law Libraries

CLIENTELE WITH VARIOUS NEEDS

For many law libraries serving courts, counties, states, or the federal government, a daily challenge is meeting the widely varying needs of the clientele. The librarian in many of these libraries is expected to help the judges, lawyers, and the public with the same level of care and diligence. His or her responsibility to all patrons does not stop with reference service, but often expands to include collection development, current awareness, and circulation policies as well. While the judge has an expert knowledge of the legal system and the research tools, the layperson inevitably does not. The law librarian in this environment must be able to switch gears rapidly to accommodate the patrons and to balance the various needs of the user groups when making acquisition decisions.

DEALING WITH THE PUBLIC

Among the difficulties facing these law librarians are dealing with the problem patron and drawing the line between legal research and legal advice. In the first instance, law librarians should look to the public library literature for guidance. Although law librarians in academic, corporate, and firm settings may also face rude or difficult patrons, they are less likely to be exposed to the dangerous or demented patron. Similarly, the law librarian who works with the public is more likely to encounter a distraught patron, perhaps looking for laws of divorce, child custody or inheritances.

Law librarians in all fields must make judgment calls to distinguish between legal research and legal advice, but those in government-sponsored libraries are probably tested more often. Anyone who deals with an inexperienced legal researcher knows how difficult it is to explain legal research methodology. Academic law librarians who work with new law school students are heavily burdened but have an easier time than those who are helping the public. Few people today understand the governmental and legal structures of this country, not to mention legislative and regulatory processes. Helping a layperson locate the necessary laws and regulations often involves a rudimentary explanation of this process and can easily cross the line to legal advice if the law librarian is not careful.

BUDGETARY CONSTRAINTS

Although many law librarians are under pressure to keep costs down, no one is more challenged to do so than the librarian of a government-sponsored law library. Federal and state governments are constantly looking for ways to reduce expenditures, and the constantly changing political contests periodically focus on library budgets. Trying to satisfy the basic needs of the various user groups with a shrinking or limited budget is no easy feat. Locating funds for computer databases, CD-ROMs, automated circulation or cataloging systems, and staff requires persuasion and external support.

SPACE LIMITATIONS

Like law libraries everywhere, space is at a premium and there is rarely any room to grow. Many government-sponsored law libraries have the added problem of being housed in an old building that was not originally designed to house a library and is not easily adapted to accommodate new technologies.

MEETING THE NEED FOR NON-LEGAL RESEARCH

Government-sponsored law libraries, like other law libraries, must begin to address the non-legal information needs of their clientele. With limited budgets there is limited funding available for general, corporate, or other traditionally non-legal reference material. Yet, as previously discussed, lawyers, judges, and scholars are increasingly forced to research the field in which the law is to be applied. Law librarians in all types of facilities must respond to these expanded research needs, and those working with small budgets must be more creative. Use of non-legal databases and cooperative lending between non-legal libraries are among the solutions to meeting the patron's needs in today's state, county, and court libraries.

General Bibliography

This selective bibliography contains an annotated list of monographs and serials for law librarians. It does not include general library literature, nor does it include literature from the legal profession. It also excludes legal research handbooks and manuals, bibliographic guides, and compilations of law books. Although many of these materials do contain useful information for law librarians, this body of information is beyond the scope of this bibliography and can be located elsewhere. For articles on particular aspects of law librarianship, please consult the bibliographies at the ends of the chapters.

AALL directory and handbook. Chicago, IL: Published for the American Association of Law Libraries by Commerce Clearing House. 1940 - . Annual.

This paperback handbook has been published since 1940 as a resource for law librarians. It contains an alphabetical list of AALL members, with geographical and firm indexes. The handbook also contains a list of the chapters, special interest sections, and committees, and it reprints the by-laws of the association. Other features include a chronology of the AALL, a list of related organizations, and an AALL publications list.

AALL newsletter. Chicago, IL: American Association of Law Libraries. v.8, Sept. 1986 - . Published monthly, except January and July.

This newsletter is free with membership to the association and serves to keep members abreast of developments within the association and the profession. Each issue generally contains a letter from the president; brief newsworthy or timely articles; news from the chapters, committees, and special interest sections; a calendar of continuing education; and membership news.

ALL newsletter. [Los Angeles, CA]: American Association of Law Libraries, Academic Law Libraries Special Interest Section. v.3(1), Nov. 1981 - .

This newsletter serves to keep the members of this division of AALL abreast of current developments and news in the field of academic law librarianship.

Altman, Devra L. *A Manual for small and medium-sized law libraries.* Chicago, IL: American Bar Foundation, 1976. 31 pages.

This brief handbook contains elementary library procedures and policies for law firms.

American Association of Law Libraries. *Introducing the American Association of Law Libraries.* Houdek, Frank G., editor. 2nd ed. Chicago, IL: Published for the American Association of Law Libraries by Lawyers Co-operative Pub. Co., 1986. 57 pages.

This brief handbook presents information on the history and organization of the American Association of Law Libraries, the professional association for law librarians in all types of law libraries.

American Association of Law Libraries. Committee on Law Library Service to Prisoners. *Recommended collections for prison and other institution law libraries.* Rev. ed. [Chicago, IL]: The Association, 1976. 8 pages.

This brief guide contains recommended minimum standards for prison and other institution law libraries.

Bowker's legal publishing preview. New York: R. R. Bowker. v.1(1), 1988 - . Published bi-monthly.

This newsletter contains a feature article followed by reviews and profiles of new print and nonprint titles in the legal field. Reviews are written by professionals in law or librarianship, while profiles are descriptive annotations provided by the publishers.

Christensen, Carol. *Law firm libraries: a selective annotated bibliography, 1959-1978.* Austin, TX: Tarlton Law Library, University of Texas School of Law, 1979. 40 pages.

This annotated bibliography is no longer up to date but presents an interesting glimpse at law firm library management during a 20-year period. The end of this period began a time of rapid growth and change for law firms and their libraries, so one could almost consider this an historical look.

The CRIV sheet. Los Angeles, CA: Committee on Relations with Information Vendors, American Association of Law Libraries. v.11(1), Sept 1988 - . Published three times a year as a supplement to the *AALL Newsletter*.

Formerly called the *Publications Clearing House Bulletin*, this newsletter aims to inform the members of the AALL of the committee's work with vendors to improve the quality of advertising, content, and related issues of legal publications and products. It is required reading for acquisitions librarians, as it also reports problems with vendor billing, false advertising claims, and marketing gimmicks.

Finley, Elizabeth. *Manual of procedures for private law libraries*. South Hackensack, NJ: Published for the American Association of Law Libraries by F. B. Rothman, 1966. 176 pages. Updated by Dyer, Susan K. *Manual of procedures for private law libraries, 1984 supplement*. Littleton, CO: Published for the American Association of Law Libraries by F. B. Rothman, 1984. 130 pages.

These handbooks are intended to serve as a basic guide to private law library operations. They contain brief chapters on nearly every phase of running a law library, with sample forms, checklists, and charts. Also included are helpful bibliographies.

Heller, James S.; Wiant, Sarah K. *Copyright handbook*. Littleton, CO: Published for the American Association of Law Libraries by F. B. Rothman, 1984. 68 pages.

This manual is a guide to copyright laws for law libraries. It includes a discussion of general principles, the owner's rights, fair use, computers and copyright, a legislative history of the law, and the impact of the laws on libraries.

Houdek, Frank G.; Goldner, Susan D. *AALL annotated meetings: an annotated index of the recordings*. Littleton, CO: F. B. Rothman, 1989 - . Loose-leaf.

This loose-leaf volume contains an index to the cassette recordings of meetings held by the American Association of Law Libraries. A review of the index provides a fascinating glimpse at the variety and scope of the interests of the association's members.

Integrated legal research: instructional techniques. Dayton, OH: Mead Data Central, Inc. v.1(1), Summer 1988 - . Published quarterly.

This newsletter, distributed as a public service by Mead Data Central to teachers of legal research in law schools, law firms, and graduate schools of library science, consists of four to eight pages of material on teaching legal research and writing. Both traditional book research and use of automated tools are included. Articles from teachers in law schools, government, and private law libraries are presented, with the focus on how research skills are or should be taught. The editor's intention is to provide "a forum for discussing the theory and practice of teaching legal research and writing." Most issues also include a brief "News & Notes" section which reports upcoming or recently held events.

International journal of legal information. Washington: Institute for International Legal Information. v.1(1) 1973 - . Published three times a year.

This journal, formerly called the *International Journal of Law Libraries*, is the official journal of the International Association of Law Libraries. Each issue presents scholarly articles on such topics as the Czechoslovakian law of joint ventures, the Belgian law of affiliation, and the European Economic Community. An excellent feature is the reviews of new periodicals and books.

The law firm library of the future: technology takes research beyond the bookshelves. New York: AM-LAW Publishing Corp., 1988. 18 pages.

This pull-out management report from the December 1988 issue of the *American Lawyer* examines the policies and practices of several large law firm libraries, with special focus on the impact of technology on traditional research and management.

Law librarianship: a handbook. Mueller, Heinz P.; Kehoe, Patrick E., editors. Littleton, CO: Published for the American Association of Law Libraries by F. B. Rothman, 1983. 2 volumes.

This two-volume manual is a comprehensive blend of practical and theoretical information on law librarianship. Organized to include everything from the history of law libraries to the impact of technology, this work is an outstanding tool for the experienced or novice law librarian.

Law libraries in Canada: essays to honour Diana M. Priestly. Fraser, Joan N., editor. Toronto: Carswell, 1988. 237 pages.

This book is a collection of articles covering the types of Canadian law libraries, research and organization of Canadian legal materials, events of historical significance to Canadian law libraries, and professional issues for law librarians.

Law library information reports. London; New York: Glanville Publishers. no.1, 1981 - . Irregular.

This series of special reports on law library administration and management is designed especially for academic law librarians. Among the titles in this series are: automation in the law school, including law libraries; planning the law library as a legal information center; microcomputer software selection for the law library; library fund-raising; insuring the law library; professional staffing and job security in the academic law library; and what law school administrators should know about the ABA/AALS law library inspection process. Many of these titles are also of interest to librarians outside of the law school environment.

Law library journal. Chicago, IL: American Association of Law Libraries. 1908 - . Published quarterly.

This journal is the official publication of the American Association of Law Libraries. It is a scholarly journal containing substantive articles on law library management, legal research tools and techniques, and related topics. Each issue contains several lengthy articles, often with excellent bibliographies. In addition, there is an outstanding "Questions & Answers" column which aims to satisfy even the most complex or exacting reference questions.

Legal information alert. Chicago, IL: Alert Information, Inc. v.1(1), 1981(?) - . Published ten times a year.

This newsletter, formerly called *U.S. Law Library Alert*, is now in its eighth year of publication. It presents "what's new in legal publications, databases and research techniques" in each 12-page issue. Among the recent feature articles are: planning for optical disk technology; hazardous waste law and research; update on LEXIS and Westlaw; and the changing field of securities law. Database news is briefly presented, and new publications are reviewed. Also included is a calendar of upcoming events for law librarians.

Legal information for the 1980's: meeting the needs of the legal profession. Taylor, Betty W., program chairperson. Littleton, CO: Published for the American Association of Law Libraries by F. B. Rothman, 1982. 593 pages.

This book is a compilation of the materials presented at the 1981 annual meeting of the American Association of Law Librarians. Although the focus of this collection is on automation, it also includes a section on the history of law libraries and legal information delivery.

Legal information management index. Newton Highlands, MA: Legal Information Services. v.1(1), Jan./Feb. 1984 - . Bi-monthly, with an annual cumulation.

This index provides keyword and author access to the hundreds of articles published by the journals and newsletters covering law librarianship. The index reviews over 115 periodicals published in the U.S. and abroad to include substantive articles, bibliographies, surveys, and reviews. This is an excellent source for locating law library-specific materials, especially useful for its coverage of AALL chapter and special interest section newsletters and for coverage of peripheral journals to which law librarians may not subscribe.

Legal information management report. Newton Highlands, MA: Legal Information Services. v.1(1), Winter 1989 - . Published quarterly.

Each issue of this new periodical addresses one area of law library management in depth. Topics covered to date are: looseleaf services selection and maintenance, billing for your services, the law librarian as a professional, and annual reports and budgets. Among the topics to be seen in future issues are: job sharing, space planning and relocation, and microform management.

Legal reference services quarterly. New York: Haworth Press. v.1(1), Spring 1981 - . Published quarterly.

Each issue of this journal contains four or more articles on legal research, reference, or the management of law libraries. Some issues are devoted to a special area of concern, such as legal bibliography, while others consist of a variety of topics. The articles vary from sharing practical experiences, reviewing reference tools, and comparing research materials to pathfinders and annotated bibliographies. Book reviews, some software and database reviews, and an occasional humorous look at law librarianship are included.

Managing the private law library 1988. French, Sharon K.; Gehringer, Susanne, co-chairpersons. New York: Practising Law Institute, 1988. 424 pages.

This course handbook, prepared for distribution at a 1988 seminar by the same name, addressed law firm library management issues of merging firms, branch libraries, corporate law libraries, and emerging technologies. Also included are statistics for law libraries and budget and cost containment issues.

Managing the private law library 1989: delivering information services. French, Sharon K.; Curci, Lucy, co-chairpersons. New York: Practising Law Institute, 1989. 552 pages.

This course handbook, prepared for distribution at a 1989 seminar by the same name, contains a variety of outlines and bibliographies on specialized legal research topics and law library management issues such as disaster planning, quality control of on-line files, and library annual reports.

Marke, Julius J.; Sloane, Richard. *Legal research and law library management.* New York: Law Journal Seminars-Press, 1982. 468 pages and pamphlet supplements.

This book consists of a series of articles that formerly appeared in the *New York Law Journal* on many aspects of legal research and law library management. Most of the articles are brief examinations of specific topics such as collection development issues, microforms, disaster planning, and legal research in New York. As such, it presents a good beginning point for setting policies and procedures and identifying areas law firms need to address.

3

Manual of law librarianship: the use and organization of legal literature. Moys, Elizabeth M., editor. 2nd ed. Boston, MA: G.K. Hall & Co., 1987. 915 pages.

This manual was published for the British and Irish Association of Law Librarians. It consists of four parts: an introduction, legal literature of the British Isles and other common law systems, legal literature of other legal systems, and law library practice. Although much of the book is devoted to the organization of legal literature, it also contains sections on general law library management, reader services, acquisitions, and cataloging and classification.

Newsletter, State, Court, & County Law Libraries SIS of the AALL. Chicago: American Association of Law Libraries State, Court, and County Law Libraries Special Interest Section. 1973 - . Published four times a year.

This newsletter for members of the special interest section of AALL contains brief articles, membership news and upcoming events, and reports on SIS business matters.

The noter up: an update service to Fundamentals of Legal Research [and] Legal Research Illustrated . . . *and a semi-annual newsletter on legal research and legal bibliography*. Dunn, Donald J., editor. Buffalo, NY: Reproduced by permission from the Foundation Press by William S. Hein & Co., 1977 - . Published semi-annually.

As the title suggests, this newsletter was originally conceived as a newsletter for professors and instructors using the legal research texts in their courses. It is also very useful as a periodic way to keep abreast of changes and new developments in legal research tools and techniques, legal writing and bibliography, and legal research instruction.

Occasional papers series. Chicago, IL: American Association of Law Libraries. Irregular.

The AALL publishes a series of papers on an irregular basis that it believes will be of interest and value to its members. Among the list of papers available are: Academic law libraries: the status of conversion to USMARC format in OCLC, RLIN and WLN; and Laserdisc technology and law libraries: selected papers from the

1987 annual meeting of the Mid-America Association of Law Libraries.

PLL perspectives. Washington: American Association of Law Libraries, Private Law Libraries Special Interest Section. v.1(1), Sept/Oct. 1988 - . Published bi-monthly.

This newsletter, which replaces the *PLL Newsletter*, focuses on issues of interest to law librarians in private law firms, corporations, and consulting. Topics are discussed briefly and are presented by practicing librarians. Each issue is approximately twenty pages in length and includes timely articles, membership and section news, and a calendar of events.

The private law firm library: an integral tool of the law firm. Wallace, Marie; Pomerantz, Julius M., co-chairpersons. New York: Practising Law Institute, 1977. 432 pages.

This course handbook, prepared for distribution at the 1977 seminar by the same name, contains articles, outlines, and bibliographies on equipping the law firm library. Intended for law librarians and law firm managers, it begins with hiring a librarian and the role of the librarian. It also includes information on planning and designing space and collection development.

Private law librarians 1986. Wallace, Marie; Wrenn, Teresa, co-chairpersons. New York: Practising Law Institute, 1986. 688 pages.

This course handbook, prepared for distribution at a 1986 seminar by the same name, is a comprehensive look at law library management issues of the 1980s. The quality of each chapter is variable, with many in outline format, but there is a great deal of information presented in the handbook.

Private law libraries: a survey of compensation, operations and collections 1990 ed. Chicago, IL: American Association of Law Libraries Private Law Libraries Special Interest Section, 1990. 59 pages.

The results of a survey of private law libraries in the United States and Canada conducted by Altman & Weil are presented in this book. While the primary focus of the survey was salary information, statistics regarding collection size, space, and on-line resources are also presented.

The private law library in the high-tech era. Strohofer, Jean; Wallace, Marie, co-chairpersons. New York: Practising Law Institute, 1983. 288 pages.

This course handbook, prepared for distribution at the 1983 seminar by the same name, contains outlines and bibliographies on law firm library management issues related to space planning, collection development, and research needs in the new age of technology.

The private law library: new information functions. Strain, Laura M., chairperson. New York: Practising Law Institute, 1981. 216 pages.

This course handbook, prepared for distribution at the 1981 seminar by the same name, contains outlines, articles, and bibliographies on private law library techniques and tools.

Private law library, 1980's and beyond. Sloane, Richard; Wallace, Marie, co-chairpersons. New York: Practising Law Institute, 1979. 320 pages.

This course handbook, prepared for distribution at a 1979 seminar by the same name, focuses on space planning and computer technology. Like all PLI course handbooks, each chapter is prepared by the speaker and may be a full-text article or an outline.

Reader in law librarianship. Reams, Bernard D., editor. Englewood, CO: Information Handling Services, Library and Education Division, 1976. 375 pages.

This book is part of the series "Readers in Librarianship and Information Science" and was recently reprinted by the William Hein Company. It includes the text of articles, addresses, essays, and lectures which were originally presented in law library literature. Although the material was written prior to 1976, many of the policies, procedures, and theories apply today, making this reader still a valuable resource.

Reader services law librarian. Chicago, IL: American Association of Law Libraries, Reader Services Special Interest Section. Published quarterly.

This brief newsletter highlights news and events of interest to law librarians who specialize in reference, research, and related reader services. Members of this special interest section of AALL receive this subscription as a benefit of membership.

Reflections on law librarianship: a collection of interviews. Littleton, CO: F. B. Rothman, 1988. 262 pages.

This collection was prepared by Marjorie A. Garson and others and was sponsored by the American Association of Law Libraries. Prominent law librarians were interviewed for their experiences, interests, and perspectives on the field of law librarianship. As a result, the compilation presents, among other things, a description of the history and development of the field, profiles of role models for others in the profession, and assistance in making the process of planning for the future somewhat clearer.

Setting the legal information action agenda for the year 2000: a workshop of the American Association of Law Libraries National Legal Resources Committee. [S.l.]: The Committee, [1988]. 2 volumes.

This two-volume set contains material presented at a conference held in October 1988. Volume One contains background reading, while Volume Two contains issues statements.

Taylor, Betty W.; Mann, Elizabeth B.; Munro, Robert J. *The 21st century: technology's impact on academic research and law libraries.* Boston, MA: G. K. Hall, 1988. 235 pages.

This handbook, part of the Professional Librarian Series, discusses automation and technological innovations in law libraries and forecasts the impact new technologies will have on the operation, financial outlook, and use of law libraries in the future.

Technical services law librarian. Los Angeles: American Association of Law Libraries Technical Services Special Interest Section. 1975 -. Published three times a year.

This newsletter is published for the Technical Services Special Interest Section and the Online Bibliographic Services Special Interest Section of the AALL. It is published to keep the members abreast of changing policies, practices, and upcoming events related to technical services and online databases.

Teitelbaum, Gene. *Inspecting a prison law library*. Holmes Beach, FL: W. W. Gaunt, 1989. 70 pages.

As the title suggests, this manual presents practical information on the standards for prison and institution law libraries.

To the partners from head librarians re law library of the year 2000. American Lawyer. Pull-out management report. New York: AM-LAW Publishing Corp., 1989. 34 pages.

This pull-out management report from the December 1989 issue of the *American Lawyer* consists of articles in the form of memos from head law librarians to their firm administration regarding the needs and expectations of law library operations in the year 2000. Among the forecasts are: 24-hour research and reference service from home via computers, increasingly complex non-legal and global research needs, and changing space needs for housing libraries.

Trends in law library management and technology. Littleton, CO: F. B. Rothman. v.1(1), July/Aug. 1987 - . Published ten times a year.

This "publication for academic, firm, corporate, and government law librarians" is a brief 8 to 10-page newsletter. Each issue contains articles written by contributing editors or other practicing librarians. Among the topics covered are: power and effective management; collection development policy statements; a disaster preparedness manual; and the future of CALR in law firms. Many articles combine practice and theory, making this an excellent tool for law library planning and development of policies and procedures.

Voges, Mickie A. *Building your law library: a step-by-step guide*. Chicago, IL: American Bar Association Section of Law Practice Management, 1988. [92] pages.

This guide is designed for the small law office or solo practitioner rather than for the trained law librarian. The book does contain organizational techniques and procedures for establishing a well-organized and maintained law collection.

Werner, Oliver James. *Manual for prison law libraries*. South Hackensack, NJ: Published for the American Association of Law Libraries by F. B. Rothman, 1976. 120 pages.

This handbook presents procedures and policies as well as required minimum standards for prison law libraries.

Index